"*How to Have an Enemy* is a powerfully disruptive book. Rejecting calls for superficial 'unity' and shallow 'forgiveness,' Melissa Florer-Bixler shows how the path to true reconciliation entails inescapable enmity, collective anger, and the dismantling of power, all fueled by a liberating love."
—**KRISTIN KOBES DU MEZ**, author of *Jesus and John Wayne*

"In *How to Have an Enemy*, Melissa Florer-Bixler reminds us that a Jesus-shaped love is not passive acceptance of everyone's opinion but a fierce movement that requires all of us to bend toward justice. This book shows us that for Melissa, the work of peace is just that: work. And she has an unflinching determination to do that work and to drag as many of us along as she can. I have no doubt she will succeed."
—**JARED BYAS**, author of *Love Matters More* and cohost of the podcast *The Bible for Normal People*

"Waging peace on a weary world that just wants to teach war or hear rumors of war, Melissa Florer-Bixler has once again declared the work of peacemaking hard, arduous, and holy. This book is a gift to those who want to gain the ability to recognize when peacemaking begins and to be open to the possibility of an end of all enemies."
—**LENNY DUNCAN** (he/him), author of *United States of Grace* and pastor of Jubilee Collective

"In a time defined by fuzzy terms like *polarization* and *division*, we are still struggling to understand what it means to live among people who wish us ill, including those in our own churches. In *How to Have an Enemy*, Melissa Florer-Bixler moves past easy ideas of peaceful coexistence and into the greater challenge of understanding how interwoven oppressions keep us entrenched in 'us and them' thinking, as well as how we need to deconstruct our own prejudices to move through simplistic ideas of division and into a more awakened consciousness. This is a book that doesn't let readers off easily, that disturbs and provokes, much like the Gospels."
—**KAYA OAKES**, journalist and author of *The Defiant Middle*

"In the face of 2020's apocalyptic revelations about the frailty of unfettered capitalism and the long-running systems of white violence comes *How to Have an Enemy*. Melissa Florer-Bixler offers expansive knowledge of

Christian and American history—particularly the long systems of racism we'd rather not acknowledge. She does not shy away, and will not allow us to, either. Yet with persistence and gentleness she holds us to the promise of resurrection we know in Jesus, with transformative conviction that we, too, might die to sin and rise to new life. Do not read this book unless you are prepared to have your soul shaken and your heart convicted."

—EMMY KEGLER, pastor, speaker, and author of *One Coin Found*

"Pastor Melissa Florer-Bixler takes us on a journey that unlocks the colonized mind, helping the reader confront the oversimplification of the gospel. She challenges us to move away from platitudes and a watered-down view of Christ's teaching and pick up the good news of transformation and liberation that causes systems of injustice to be broken apart. This book is a call to action for the church of today, a powerful tool to help rescue the good news from those who seek to use its words to oppress and hold people in spiritual bondage."

—GLEN GUYTON, executive director of Mennonite Church USA and author of *Reawakened*

"Jesus called his followers to love their enemies, but this commandment has been weaponized to pacify Christians in the face of injustice. Melissa Florer-Bixler's *How to Have an Enemy* will transform your understanding of this foundational Christian idea. She guides us past the mollifying interpretation of Jesus' words and reveals how enemy-love supports the work of liberation."

—GUTHRIE GRAVES-FITZSIMMONS, author of *Just Faith*

"*How to Have an Enemy* draws on the poetry of Scripture to empower us to name and call out our enemies as Jesus did. In challenging us to redefine the principles of a judicial system that targets and disproportionately punishes bodies of color, Melissa Florer-Bixler creates a new lens through which to observe our enemies, intimately drawing us closer to the other in a manner that invites lament, reconnection, and repentance towards healing and rightful justice. This book is essential for a country divided by an era of opposition."

—GRACE JI-SUN KIM, professor of theology at Earlham School of Religion and author of *Hope in Disarray*

HOW TO HAVE AN ENEMY

RIGHTEOUS ANGER & THE WORK OF PEACE

MELISSA FLORER-BIXLER

Herald
P R E S S

Harrisonburg, Virginia

Herald Press
PO Box 866, Harrisonburg, Virginia 22803
www.HeraldPress.com

Study guides are available for many Herald Press titles at
www.HeraldPress.com.

HOW TO HAVE AN ENEMY
© 2021 by Herald Press, Harrisonburg, Virginia 22803. 800-245-7894.
   All rights reserved.
Library of Congress Control Number: 2021936512
International Standard Book Number: 978-1-5138-0813-0 (paperback),
   978-1-5138-0814-7 (hardcover), 978-1-5138-0815-4 (ebook)
Printed in the United States of America
Cover and interior design by Merrill Miller

Unless otherwise noted, Scripture text is quoted, with permission, from the
New Revised Standard Version, © 1989, Division of Christian Education of
the National Council of Churches of Christ in the United States of America.
Scripture quotations marked "KJV" are taken from the *King James Version*. All
references from the Talmud are from Koren Noé Talmud. Sanhedrin 98a. The
William Davidson digital edition of the Koren Noé Talmud, with commentary
by Rabbi Adin Steinsaltz Even-Israel. Digital. https://www.korenpub.com.

Chapter 3, "Praying for Enemies," originally appeared as "No One Will Take
Responsibility for Faye Brown's Death." Reprinted with permission from
Sojourners, 800-714-7474, www.sojo.net.

25 24 23 22 21   10 9 8 7 6 5 4 3 2 1

Contents

*"Justice shall march in the forefront,
and peace shall follow the way."*

PSALM 85:13 rendered from *The Revised Grail Psalms*[1]

Foreword

DARING TO LIVE the truth of the gospel is a peculiar and disorienting endeavor. America has always been at odds with the gospel. It wants the notoriety but cannot stomach the demand, as Melissa Florer-Bixler articulates, "to enfold our lives into the gospel, our whole lives."

This challenge to enfold our essence into a narrative that is counter to our proclivity toward predatory self-interest is a difficult virtue to accept. American forms of "faith"—I must place faith in quotes because our national religion is not the Judeo-Christian tradition often lauded by pundits and marketers of the American mythos—are a mix of market desires and spiritual rhetoric clothed in ecclesiastical garments. Our national religious project fails to force humanity to face the complicity and collective injury we inflict upon ourselves and each other. This enfolding makes a demand on the human vessel to be seen as enemy and friend, broken and blessed, oppressor and oppressed, affirming and phobic. Our national religion needs "others" or "enemies" wrapped in xenophobic language to hold on to the crumbling myth of superiority.

Our national "faith" is one of the entrenched stumbling blocks of the American project. This "faith" dismisses Black Lives Matter as division, Colin Kaepernick as unpatriotic, transgender rights as undermining culture, police abolition as a communist plot, and critical race theory as antithetical to the gospel. This "faith" driven by fear of difference was demonstrated publicly with boisterous arrogance covered in ignorance when several presidents of Southern Baptist seminaries in a joint statement "proclaimed" critical race theory as incompatible with the gospel. It should be noted, these same seminaries were either silent or accepting of slavery, silent or accepting of Jim Crow laws, and never uttered one word to support families of Black and brown citizens who died at the hands of police whom their tax dollars support.

In this book, Melissa Florer-Bixler offers our nation an opportunity to reclaim a Jesus-centered gospel instead of a market-driven "faith" we knowingly and unknowingly practice. As a scholar, theologian, minister, and conjuror of holy mischief, she challenges us to face the enemy. This enemy is us. We collectively as a nation have dishonored the gospel, creating a "golden calf" of false patriotism and myths of racial caste. We are the enemy; the enemy who uses the rhetoric of freedom, but practices policies that negate human agency. We are the enemy, and in order to be saved from ourselves, we must enfold our broken lives into the gospel in order to witness the world anew.

How to Have an Enemy is a book we need as a community of faith and as a nation. Though it is written from the balcony of the Christian spiritual practice, this book speaks to the diverse and varied spiritual topography of our nation. Pastor

Florer-Bixler is unafraid to examine sources outside her tradition to gain insight into the blind spots that Americanized "faith" practitioners create.

Years ago, when I graduated from seminary, I had my first confrontation with a white evangelical who could not understand why I was reading Malcolm X. He was convinced my reading choice was un-American and my calling as a minister was now in jeopardy because I had the audacity to read the words of a Black Muslim. I think of that moment often, because I failed miserably to respond with my life enfolded into the gospel. If Florer-Bixler's work were in my hand, I might have discovered "how to have an enemy" and created a pathway to what Rev. Dr. Samuel DeWitt Proctor stated to his congregation at the Abyssinian Baptist Church in Harlem, New York: "I learned I do not have enemies, just confused friends." When we enfold our whole lives into the gospel, we catch a glimpse of the sacred in all humanity, even the most broken among us.

It is my prayer that this book you now hold will help you enfold your life into the gospel, and that you will discover that, as our ancestor Dr. Proctor stated, we have no enemies, just confused friends.

—Rev. Dr. Otis Moss III, senior pastor of
Trinity United Church of Christ in Chicago

Gratitude as Preface

THIS IS A BOOK ABOUT enemies, Jesus, and how the church is ordered by reconciliation. I'll begin with a few words about the church and the people who shaped my life and my thoughts over the decades that I have been asking how to "love my enemies," even as I watch enemies work toward my destruction and that of people, cultures, and places that I love.

First, a word about the church. In each period of history since at least the eleventh century, different iterations of Christianity have attempted to seize control as history's winners and deciders. Our world bears the scars—from the Crusades to the Inquisition. The wounds are fresh in our own time, from the violence of Christian nationalism's attempted coup at the U.S. Capitol, to legislation that allows religious organizations to control women's access to birth control, whether these women are religiously against the use of contraception or not. In the vision of history that shapes a narrative of Christian nationalism, two entities vie for control—the church and the world—and only the church can rightly order society. Those outside the church must be brought, by coercion, if necessary, into this order.

I offer gratitude to Kathryn Tanner who offered me a theology without Christian conquering.[1] Tanner's theology provides an "undefensive" posture of the church toward the broader social order. The center of Tanner's theology is this: "God wants to give us the fullness of God's own life through the closest possible relationship with us as that comes to completion in Christ."[2] The church's purpose is directed toward the blessings, wholeness, and peace of all creation.

As a people who orient our lives toward imitation of the triune God, the church is "essentially relational."[3] Our purpose as followers of Jesus is found in shared concerns and commitments to solidarity and humility. We do not need to be in competition with the gifts of creation, nor do we need to dominate those beyond the church. Our Christian identity "is no longer a matter of unmixed purity, but a hybrid affair established through unusual uses of materials found elsewhere."[4] We construct Christian meaning through movements, philosophies, and insights that we borrow. These ideas become illuminating for our lives as Christians when they are "twisted and turned, used in different ways, when set in a new [Christian] context."[5] This process is messy and vulnerable. It necessitates forms of life that can sustain "a genuine community of argument" set at a common task, rather than unifying around a disembodied set of doctrines.[6]

My second gratitude is extended to the late Dr. James Cone. Cone helped me understand a theology of two orders: the order of sin and death, and the order of liberation and redemption. These movements pass through all social locations, including

the church. In his writings I learned how the old order is constituted in the life, death, and resurrection of Jesus, and I learned
to take seriously that "any theology that is indifferent to the
theme of liberation is not Christian theology."[7] The church is
not capable of sealing itself off from the powers of destruction
and death. Instead of naming an exterior "empire" at which to
direct our enmity, Cone confronts the church at the place of
its collaboration with the sin of white supremacy. The church
is porous not only to the wisdom of others but also to collaboration with the principalities and powers of death.

Following Tanner's theological determination that God
gives gifts freely and actively to all creation rather than simply mediating those gifts through the church, I give thanks for
those outside the church who provide the cultural materials to
generate new ways of life that build a world of liberation. My
first gratitude is to Kimberlé Crenshaw, whose work on intersectionality shaped my theology and activism.

Crenshaw's work began with the legal insight that the oppressions experienced by Black women could not be catego-
rized solely through the lens of anti-Black racism or white
feminism. Instead, Black women faced oppression at the
juncture, or intersection, of race and gender. This insight revealed the interconnectedness of other oppressions. Ageism,
homophobia, Islamophobia, sexism, racism, ableism—these
oppressions are interrelated and thrive off the same economic
and social powers where straight, white, Christian, temporarily
able-bodied men are the norm against which all others are defined. There is no hierarchy of oppressions. Rather, many people experience multiple oppressions simultaneously. The call to
dismantle one oppression will inevitably lead to the work of
dismantling the others.

After the death of Trayvon Martin at the hands of a vigilante, the Black Lives Matter movement called us as a country toward a movement to dismantle the legacies of oppression that run through our social order. This was a movement that centered the experiences of Black, queer people—a "leader-full" movement, "inclusive and spacious."[8] I am grateful to queer Black women who were the beating heart of the Movement for Black Lives, and I name the movement's cofounders: Alicia Garza, Opal Tometi, and Patrisse Cullors.

Describing the Black Lives Matter movement, Garza writes,

> When we say Black Lives Matter, we are talking about the ways in which Black people are deprived of our basic human rights and dignity. It is an acknowledgement that Black poverty and genocide is state violence. It is an acknowledgment that 1 million Black people locked in cages in this country—one half of all people in prisons or jails—is an act of state violence.[9]

Black queer people bear additional burdens in hetero-patriarchy, Black girls bear the additional burden of sexualization, and Black disabled people bear the additional burden of racialized eugenics. Black people bear burdens in specific ways because the United States grows roots in the soil of white supremacy.

Garza's vision is not for a new racial hierarchy with Black people on top. She envisions a world of freedom from oppression altogether. "We're not saying Black lives are more important than other lives, or that other lives are not criminalized and oppressed in various ways," she says.[10] Because poverty, criminalization, and sexualization are rooted in the subjugation of Black bodies, when we attend to these issues as they uniquely impact the Black community, we are all lifted up.

The call of the church is to align ourselves with movements like Black Lives Matter and those patterned in similar struggles for liberation (Chicano/Latinx liberation, LGBTQ liberation, disability liberation). The church as a historical, sociological entity has been an abject failure at this project. The line we trace back through the centuries shows us little about Jesus and a great deal about the victors of church-state history—the powerful who were able to align themselves with and coordinate within coercive, violent state power. Evangelicalism and its election of Donald Trump is the most recent signpost on this long road of coercive power-keeping.

In orienting my life toward the church my next gratitude is to Karl Barth. Barth, alongside my inculturation into the Mennonite church, embedded my faith in Jesus, "slain from the foundation of the world" (Revelation 13:8 KJV). From Barth I learned that "the world would be lost without Jesus Christ, His word and work. . . . The world would not necessarily be lost without the church."[11] With Peter Dula, I understand that the church is occasional, occurring from time to time, rather than a product that can be traced in linear fashion through history. Sometimes the church is the space of intimacy between two or three people, sometimes an episodic and rare political response to the call of Jesus. So, thank you, also, to Peter.[12]

I have been inordinately lucky to find my way into classrooms and before teachers who taught me well and gave me good books to read. Thanks to Ivy George, who assigned Thandeka to my class on postcolonial feminism while I was still a teenager and assured that my racial education included grappling with my whiteness. Gratitude goes to Daniel Johnson, whose class in critical theory introduced me to Foucault, Gramsci, Weber, and Marx, and provided a sure intellectual foundation. Gratitude to

Yolanda Pierce, Willie Jennings, Mark Lewis Taylor, Joel Marcus, and Stanley Hauerwas, who have been wise and gifted teachers.

I write because I have questions and imagine that, perhaps, others would like to think alongside me. I wrote this particular book out of discontent with my own tradition's response to the Trump administration. This book is my cantankerous act of love for my church because I want the Mennonite church to live into the fullness of God's reign. As it is, this book is suited for people who make claims to a shared commitment of following Jesus. I don't have an agenda for society at large or even ecumenical dialogue. As a Mennonite I am a localist when it comes to church, and I hope this book will be helpful for congregations who grapple with unity and difference.

— — —

I WROTE THIS BOOK in the last year of the Trump administration. The years of this administration were years of terror. I was afraid every day—for myself, for my friends, for people who I cared for and loved and pastored. And yet, that fear was with intention, over decades. I live in a country created for my flourishing. Throughout the history of the United States, the preservation and protection of women like me, white women, is one of the primary excuses given by white supremacists and their institutions to degrade and suppress Black and brown people.

I refuse to submit to or live out this racial fraud. Instead, I work to cultivate a life that removes me from the kind of life in which white people "imagine themselves as spectators of racial suffering and observers of black pain who are allowed to feel only assorted forms of white guilt," as Willie Jennings writes. My commitment is sustained and ongoing, a lifetime of working toward our mutual liberation, slowly unraveling the long line of oppressions that are knit into my life and connected to the world.

I am grateful to all those whose writing and activism, often over decades, has sustained in me a hopeful imagination and slowly built new paths for a new world to be realized: Barbara Smith, Ruby Sales, Angela Y. Davis, Rufina Amaya, Keeanga-Yamahtta Taylor, adrienne maree brown, and Mariame Kaba. I am grateful for the women of the Mennonite church who went before and walk beside me, among them Juanita Lark and Rowena Lark, Esther Hinojosa, Sue Park-Hur, Regina Shands Stoltzfus, Michelle Armster, and Iris de León-Hartshorn. I am also grateful for the people who have become my organizing community, working toward common liberation in the creation of memorials to lynching victims in Wake County, the removal of Confederate monuments, and establishing a citizen review board for police. I extend my gratitude to the organizers and co-conspirators of ONE Wake, Emancipate NC, and Southerners on New Ground. I have been sustained by the common work, activism, and purpose of these relationships.

I offer gratitude to those who read this manuscript at various stages and offered their response—my parents, Michael Gonzalez, Isaac Villegas, and Lori Baron. Special thanks to my editor, Elisabeth Ivey, and to Amy Gingerich and Meghan Florian at Herald Press.

I am grateful for the people who have been the source of fleeting moments of church. For Gwyneth, who has carried joy and pain with me for half a lifetime. For my parents, who rooted me in love and hope. For my family, especially my children—Etta, Wick, and Tennyson. For Raleigh Mennonite Church, where I am a priest among priests, and where the flare of the fugitive burns unexpectedly, with warmth and power.

ONE

Who Is My Enemy?

TWO MEN IN UNIFORM make their way toward one another across the frozen ground, the stars lighting the way before them. At first they are tentative. The air is acrid with gunpowder and the stench of burning skin. After a few steps the men's strides lengthen as their confidence grows. They pace across the gray landscape, ruined by ash and blood. The soldiers stand silent before one another as their hearts pump with the adrenaline of fear and suspicion. One of the men pulls something from his pocket. "Fröhliche Weihnachten," he says with a weary grin. He hands the French soldier a cigar.

The World War I Christmas Day truce is a fabled moment in the history of enemies. The 2004 film *Joyeux Noel* is one of many depictions of the brief armistice between the German, French, and Scottish soldiers that took place on Christmas Day in the middle of the war. On screen men laid down their weapons to play football and sing carols on Christmas morning. It's a story that is told over and over from pulpits and in storybooks to remind us how face-to-face contact—how knowing one another—can bring peace to enemies. "To die tomorrow," says one of the actor soldiers in *Joyeux Noel*, "is even more absurd than dying yesterday."[1]

In the myth of the Christmas Day truce, it is the soldiers who devise the armistice, eager to thwart officers who can't see the pointlessness of the war. Once the truce ends and the commanding officers take control of the situation, the soldiers who laughed and smoked cigars with their enemies refuse to pick up their guns again. The army is forced to move new troops to the front lines and the defecting soldiers are punished. Despite the costs enmity gives way to friendship, and war has no place in the hearts of soldiers who experienced the miracle of the Christmas Day truce.

— — —

I HEAR PEOPLE evoke the power of the Christmas Day cease-fire in today's divided political climate, where I am told polarization both in and outside the church walls is at a new and unique zenith in history. People of goodwill lament this stratification, the widening gap between ideological positions, with no middle ground for negotiation. I hear these people mourn that we've hardened into camps, often described as "left" and "right," and that these allegiances set our primary identities. We can no longer understand one another.

In this way of addressing conflict and division, it is Christ, not our politics, that gives us hope. If we knew each other, if we reached across the political divide toward our unity in Jesus, we could stamp out our false enmity. Early in my pastorate, I served churches that participated in a communion service on Election day. At noon, after going to the polling station to vote, we would gather to share the Lord's Supper. The organization that promoted this service encouraged churches to embrace our unity in Jesus. No matter whom we supported in the voting booth, we left behind political identities at the door of the church. Here before the table of Christ, we were one and Jesus was Lord.

What I couldn't see at the time, what I learned after sustained formation in the work of anti-oppression, was that these churches—primarily upper-middle class and white—would thrive no matter who was elected to national office. At the end of the day we were largely unaffected by the outcome. This was not the case for others for whom "politics" would determine the quality of their children's schools; their community's access to food, transportation, clean water, and jobs; and whether they would gain citizenship, earn a living wage, or receive health care. What kind of unity did we have if we were not united around their welfare, if we did not see their thriving as our own thriving?

It turns out this kind of unity—the kind that was achieved in ritual but not replicated in life—was a myth. We keep these myths alive because they offer the convenience of personal transformation over the difficult and costly work of excavating the deep roots that feed conflicts between enemies. These roots must be pulled up before we can begin to talk of reconciliation or unity. We declare "Jesus is Lord" by ripping out the systems of death and destruction that dominate our lives, and by planting something new in their place.

As it turns out the Christmas Day ceasefire of World War I was not an epiphany of anti-war resistance often portrayed in popular culture. Officers, not soldiers, planned the truce in advance. The soldiers who participated were not punished for participating. While the truce is often portrayed as a secret, meant to hide the possibilities of peace from the public, records show information about the day was widely available. But most significant is that the men who participated in the truce readily picked up their weapons on December 26. They returned to battle against the soldiers they'd met the previous day.

The truce was significant for the men involved and many wrote home to share with loved one about the momentous relief the ceasefire provided. Soldiers were able to rebuild the trenches. The men buried their dead. Some ventured out to meet enemy soldiers and to learn more about them. [2] This was likely one spark among many in building resistance to war. But the truth of this moment is complicated. Empathy, friendship, and kindness are powerful forces. But so is war. It would take more than an encounter with the enemy to unravel the entrenched political drama that led to a world at arms. There are few easy solutions to working out enmity.

Rather than idealizing a single moment of empathy, I'm struck by the stories of German citizens and soldiers who committed themselves to organized and often dangerous acts of rebellion against the imperialist war that embroiled the world. One of those moments came in October of 1918, when German naval soldiers were commanded to fire on the British in a last attempt to stem the tide of the war. Five times in a row they refused to obey the order. One thousand soldiers were arrested as a result. [3] Over the course of the war socialists and Christian pacifists resisted. They were a significant force in ending the Great War as they engaged in sustained and costly action. Ordinary people organized to interrogate the economic, political, and social powers of imperialism. [4]

— — —

WE ARE INVESTED in the myth of instantaneous friendship across enemy lines as a cure to our social ills because it offers a simple explanation for the troubles we face today. The trouble, according to this theory, is that we have divided the world into "us and them." Once we divide up the world in this way—into friends and enemies—we are destined for binary thinking that leads to intractable conflict. To make matters worse, the only way to sustain our identity in these "tribes" is to believe in our rightness and with equal ferocity in the wrongness of the other. To believe we are correct over and against others is the height of self-righteousness. This failure to disassociate our faith from our political lives is called tribalism. We can remedy tribalism with open-mindedness to the complicated nature of individual human beings; we can listen across the divides to see what we can create in a new space outside "politics as usual."

The language of tribalism, as well as the fears it communicates, contains its own genealogy. Rowan Williams reminds us of the sobering roots of this language: "The very word 'tribalism' tells a story, about the demeaning or marginalising of cultures that we call 'tribal.'"[5] In the era of colonial expansion, certain kinds of behavior and beliefs were deemed normative by European settlers. Other ways of being, thinking, acting, and relating were interesting or novel but ultimately "doomed and deviant."[6] The rational, enlightened group—those with the gold and guns—would ensure the extinction of those who would not conform.

"Tribalism," writes Williams, describes ways of life that are "aberrations from the norm."[7] Colonizers deemed the people they encountered on their journeys of empire expansion as lacking the moral and ethical skills to govern themselves. Eventually these white settlers would force upon Indigenous peoples a universal set of values that they deemed superior, established in the rational and scientific. European colonization determined and policed the boundaries of acceptable difference in economics, family, religion, and education.

European settlers implemented their social order through the sword and the gun. The "taming" of tribalism was devastating for the survival of Indigenous peoples and their cultures. Native boarding schools set their purpose on "killing the Indian" to force into existence a new citizen, one who would contribute to the economic and political vibrancy of the colonized nation. This Enlightenment rationality was, they claimed, universal. Non-Europeans had the choice to conform or be destroyed. "Genocide," writes Williams, "can wear the dress of benign progressivism, *as well as* that of murderous violence."[8]

Who determines what is reasonable difference and what causes rupture? Who defines the center of our identity, one that pushes aside questions that are considered divisive politics by some but are life or death to others? Who is this Jesus around whom we center our identity? These are not pedantic questions. They are questions that, when we fail to ask them, invite well-reasoned and thoughtful destruction of those at the margins of power.

— — —

THE WORK OF THE CHURCH is not to unify as a way to negate difference or to overcome political commitments. Instead, we are called to enfold our lives into the gospel, our *whole* lives. The good news of Jesus Christ is only good news when it proclaims that we will overcome enmity by aligning ourselves with others who reject the principalities and powers of the old age, knowing this will set us all free.

It is easier and more convenient to reduce our conflicts to misunderstandings between individuals or quarrels that we can overcome by establishing relationships or by gaining new information. Framing enmity as an issue solely between individuals, rather than dependent upon systemic and coercive power, is popular in and outside the church. In the United States, police departments host events built on this premise. In my city officers meet at McDonald's, a favored youth hangout. Officers sit at tables and hand out one-dollar gift certificates. They share soda and ice cream with patrons. They hand out yellow sheriff badge stickers to children. Most of the time these events happen in historically Black neighborhoods in Raleigh, where tensions between police and civilians run high.

The theory at work behind these events is that relationships will mitigate community tensions with the police. If people knew each other, the theory goes, if they sat down and heard each other's stories, heard from a different perspective, they would be changed. The anger, hatred, and frustration would dissolve into compassion because the two conflicting parties encountered the humanity of one another. The next time police and young people met, under duress, the situation would more likely resolve in a positive way because of the relationship established prior.

We are told this is the moral compass that guides police-community relations, and people apply this form of conflict resolution globally. Relationship holds the power to prevent violence. But it is a force both limited and complicated. When I hear that police show up at McDonald's to meet Black youth, I have no doubt that Black parents and caregivers are giving their kids "the talk," a reality of Black childhood, to balance out these encounters.

"I'll never forget there was a time—the kids wanted to go to the park," Kenya Young told a radio host about giving her three Black sons "the talk":

> I remember the kids asking to go to the park and the laundry list of what I had to tell them: "Don't wear your hood. Don't put your hands in your pocket. If you get stopped, don't run. Put your hands up. Don't make a lot of moves. Tell them your mother works for NPR." I mean, it just went on and on.[9]

Young's instructions to her sons remind us that empathic moments of personal engagement with police are dangerous for Black children. Instead, caregivers and trusted adults explain that the police have an implicit bias against Black people, especially Black men and boys. "The truth of the matter is no matter what we do, what job we get, what college we go to, what education we have, what level we are, how much money, what car," Young explains, "anything that you think may change even a little bit about how people see you, there are still people that are only going to see the skin color."[10] In their encounters, police will treat her Black children differently than their white peers, often assuming they are older and more aggressive. On the shoulder of a dark highway, it doesn't matter if they met once at a McDonald's.

"The talk" does not erase the humanity of a police officer. Instead, Black parents share it as a tool for survival. Often missing in the schools of conflict resolution that depend on empathy as their primary tool is an accurate assessment of power. The assumption that all our struggles boil down to misunderstanding negates that parties in conflict do not come with equal access to power over their lives. The attempt to resolve conflict with interpersonal strategies like empathy often disregards how coercion and force shape the lives of enemies.

We see this power inequity in policing. And we need a new culture, not relationships, to address this inequity. Those of us doing the work of police abolition—the collective movement toward a world freed from the structures of a coercive force called the police—believe officers are doing precisely the work they are expected to do. Police officers may take up this role thinking they keep people safe, that they support the wholeness of the community. They think they stop bad people from hurting good people. In reality the problem with policing is not a few bad officers who need retraining but policing itself.

Police are given permission to enact violence in order to keep in place a form of life that the state determines to be good. We often think of police as a presence to uphold the law. But the law exists within the larger account of the kind of society we expect police to maintain. A country where white supremacy runs in the roots will produce white supremacist outcomes. Over and over, throughout the history of the United States, the interpretation and enforcement of laws benefit some (white people) at the expense of others (everyone else).

The Movement for Black Lives that calls to defund the police is not about hatred for police, hatred for orderly social life, or hatred for safety. It is a matter of changing the way that we attend to the system at the center of human conflict. Rather than focusing on training individual officers, the call of abolitionists is to leave behind the logic of policing itself. Holding events where citizens get to know the police does not produce the structural change needed to keep Kenya Young's children—and all Black children—safe from police encounters. Interpersonal connection is an unhelpful distraction. In the hands of police it is propaganda. This propaganda, in the form of goodwill gestures by police and humorous videos, plays on feelings of empathy in order to sidetrack the documented, systemic racism and violence of policing in the United States.

— — —

POWER SEPARATES difference from enmity. I use the language of enemies in this book to describe a relationship between people, one that recognizes how a person uses their power, actively or passively, to harm or dominate another. When there are enemies, one is in power over the other, or there is a conflict over who holds power.[11] Power is not bad. We need power to act. Exercising power is how we make our lives better. We need power to make choices and to assure our thriving. But calls to Christian unity that ignore the dynamics of racial, gendered, and class power end with devastating consequences.

As it is not every conflict is one of enmity. We can misconstrue who our enemies are. We can falsely assess our power and that of our supposed enemy. We do not always rightly gauge tolerable difference. We see in the United States where Christian nationalists claim persecution and rally around religious freedom. A closer look reveals that the real issue is not being persecuted or actively harmed. It is assenting to live by the mutual agreements made for the thriving of all people in a pluralistic society. Christian nationalists fear losing control of the power they have held for centuries—religious power intertwined with white supremacist power—or even the prospect of sharing this power with others. Those who have amassed structural power worry about the tables being turned, with white people on the losing end of history, relegated to the bottom of the hierarchy of structural power. In order to understand enmity rightly we are required to distinguish between the fear of losing power and the fear of being harmed.

The discomfort Christian nationalists feel when a moment of silence replaces a Christian prayer in schools is not equivalent to Black people's experiences of white supremacy in virtually every facet of life, from healthcare to education to policing. Until we are willing to name, assess, and address power—how we come to the church in bodies that bear within them legacies of power brokering, centering, and divestment—our Christian unity is little more than a strategy to maintain the status quo and avoid conflict.

Instead, we are called to the reign of God. The renewed order of Jesus' reign of love and peace is not designed for the destruction of anyone. As long as there are victims, there are victimizers. As long as there are oppressors, they will act on the oppressed. Our struggles are intertwined. Our participation in the destructive force of violence and death leads to our mutual ruin. When we answer the call to the interconnectedness of our struggles, of our ability to participate in the world as both victim and victimizers, the good news has found its way to us.

In critiques of Black Lives Matter, I often encounter confusion regarding the vision of the movement and how those who participate imagine the future. I have witnessed white people dismiss Black Lives Matter because they assume the movement vaunts one identity over another, inverting a racial hierarchy that my ancestors created and white supremacist powers in our systems maintain. But Black Lives Matter excises these patterns of dominance. The experience of Black America is exceptional, explains Alicia Garza. Black communities bear a unique burden of state-sponsored white supremacy, "and the fact that the lives

of Black people—not ALL people—exist within these conditions is a consequence of state violence."[12] But Garza continues:
"*When Black people get free, everybody gets free.*"

"We understand that when Black people in this country get
free, the benefits will be wide reaching and transformative for
society as a whole," writes Garza.[13]

> As people who have our minds stayed on freedom, we can
> learn to fight anti-Black racism by examining the ways in
> which we participate in it, even unintentionally, instead of
> the worn out and sloppy practice of drawing lazy parallels
> of unity between peoples with vastly different experiences
> and histories.[14]

No community, no person, no society can be free until Black
communities are free to express outrage, until that outrage is
met as an invitation to transformation through solidarity, and
until white people lay down our weapons of economic and environmental terror, of policing and surveillance, and commit
ourselves to our corporate freedom. This is the unity to which
Christians are called.

— — —

THE WORK OF PEACE that begins with the transformation of
structures of power stands in stark contrast to calls for unity
that purport to overcome a category called "politics." Our mutual participation in the destruction of ourselves and our neighbors, and our redemption from these cycles of violence, is the
heart of the gospel. In Jesus, we come to know that there are no
"pure victims." We are, each of us, both victims and victimizers.
No group, people, or individual is freed from harming others
and being the recipients of harm.

The movement of God's reign ends this human struggle. But this does not happen by reducing, overlooking, or denying the structural power that aligns within our bodies. Instead, the good news of Jesus Christ attends to and dismantles the ways this power shapes our personal relationships and corporate life. "Harm is a basic fact of human reality. We can't avoid harm and harming others," writes Amanda Aguilar Shank.[15] But we can begin to attend to the systems that respond to this harm by perpetuating injury and passing the damage on to those who harmed.

It is Jesus who establishes accountability without punishment and justice without coercion. Jesus' refusal to engage or reform a regime of coercion is a shock to those around him. He has little patience for those who limit the possibility of transformation. He is intolerant of righteousness that places a burden on the poor. He astonishes his followers with interpretations of the law that are impossible to uphold. And through this ministry Jesus disrupts and reimagines the social and political order.

Jesus does not take time to understand the position of the teachers of the law. He shows no interest in cultivating empathy for Roman officials. He stands silent before Pilate's attempt to discover a reason to set Jesus free. Jesus refuses to lure anyone in or to convince them of his position. He heals and teaches, invites and shares meals among those who already bear within them the reign of God. He becomes a new creation, and he invites those who wish to join it to leave behind their old lives and follow him.

Jesus stands outside the violence and coercion of a social order of sin and eventually becomes its victim. It is in Jesus' life, death, and resurrection that we are ushered into a world where our lives are no longer defined by the enmity but by the possibility of enmity's end. If we construe this as shared morality, pietistic withdrawal from the world, or a reform movement, we truncate the power of the gospel as the renewal of "all things."

The good news of Jesus Christ is for the redemption of the world, for victims and victimizers, for oppressed and oppressors, for the way destruction is borne in each of us. The gospel is good news for the mother who catches her breath each time her Black child walks out the door, afraid of a deadly encounter with a cop. The gospel is good news for ICE agents who need to be saved from destruction to themselves and others. The gospel is good news for the person without immigration papers, awaiting deportation. We are freed from the logic of death, from the gods of scarcity and violence, from a politics where some prosper at the expense of others, and from the fear behind power, control, and coercion that are the operational center of the old order.

Because of this, unity is not a matter of morally getting on the same page, verbal assent to creedal formulas, or sharing the same meal around the table. Instead, in the New Testament, salvation is knit together as a new social and economic order, what in this book I will, from time to time, call the reign of God. In the Bible, to be healed of physical illness is to be forgiven of sin. Household economics are parables to describe salvation. Meals that establish patron-client relationships are upended to reveal a new, lifegiving social order. We come to learn that our redemption from sin and death is also redemption from the devastation and violence we enact on one another.

TWO

Making Room for Enemies

THE SUNDAY AFTER the 2016 election of Donald Trump, our church mourned. For months we'd shared our anxiety about the rising tide of white nationalism in the presidential campaign. We were horrified as we watched candidate Trump mock a disabled reporter and stoke racist fears about Mexican people. Women in my congregation who had survived sexual assault were alarmed when Republicans shrugged off a tape in which candidate Trump bragged about committing sexual assault. Our church feared that the misogyny, homophobia, ableism, and racism that was being fomented in massive crowds across the country would become policy. When this came to fruition in the general election, we showed up bleary eyed to the worship service to ask God for help. We needed to be together in our fear and confusion.

Because we follow Jesus, because we are told in the Gospels that we meet God in the dispossessed, we were terrified by what this election would mean for undocumented people, for Black people, for disabled people, for LGBTQ people—people who make up our church. Because we love them—because they are us—we grieved and raged against an election that validated an undercurrent of hatred running below the surface of public respectability. We read psalms of lament and psalms of angry protest. We prayed for God's deliverance. But we did not pray for unity with Christians who supported the Republican candidate.

I didn't consider if a Trump supporter might be in worship that morning in November, offended by the prayers and tears. It didn't matter. We needed a space to mourn—a place of safety and refuge, a space of shared anger. I was trained that, despite the risk to job security, the work of pastors is not to soften strong beliefs or to shelter oppressive ideology under the guise of our oneness in Christ. Instead, it is our work to carve out a common life within the good news of Jesus' redemption.

Living out this good news is not simple or straightforward. Our church is made of people. We, too, carry within us particular histories along lines of class, gender, sexuality, and race. A majority-white congregation, we are constantly undergoing the work of repentance and return for our individual and collective enmeshment in white supremacy. As a church that includes a broad spectrum of socioeconomic classes, we pay attention to how money shapes power in our church and our lives and how we can redistribute what we have. Some of us embody, simultaneously, identities and genealogies that grant us historic power and marginalization. Our lives are complicated by sin. But we have developed habits and disciplines of discernment that help us, most of the time, to live faithfully in the midst of conflict.

We work together to differentiate what is tolerable from what is insupportable. Once we have discerned, we hold one another accountable for the kind of life we are committed to living.

We learn this from the Bible. In the New Testament we discover a church that put socially marginal people at the center of their lives and worked together to discern how Jesus was acting in and through them to be good news for all of creation. In the Bible we encounter people who labor to dismantle class and social hierarchies embedded in their cultures and to distribute their wealth among one another. We see people who reject coercion and violence as the tools of an old order, even though it will cost them their lives. A tax collector bankrupts himself to undo the economic tyranny that characterized his profession. Conversely a rich man deserts the mission of Jesus because he cannot give up his wealth.

Reconciliation that offers healing and hope pulls us out of amorphous and power-obscuring centrism and into new cultures of solidarity and self-/communal-discovery. One formative movement that offers insight into the importance and power of identity-based movements is the Combahee River Collective, organized around the flourishing of Black, queer women in the 1960s. In the 1960s, as today, white feminists aligned their political interests with white men at the cost of Black women's liberation. At the same time, Barbara Smith and the other members of the collective recognized sexism and homophobia in the mainstream movement for civil rights. The women of Combahee carved out political space that attended to the multiplicity of their identities and how those identities intersected and intertwined.

Combahee formed a space for activism and liberation around what Kimberlé Crenshaw would later call intersectionality,

"The idea that multiple oppressions reinforce each other to create new categories of suffering."[1] The section on the Combahee River Collective Statement on beliefs begins, "Above all else, our politics initially sprang from the shared belief that Black women are inherently valuable, that our liberation is a necessity not as an adjunct to somebody else's but because of our need as human persons for autonomy."[2] The most potent and radical politics, the statement continues, "come directly out of our own identity, as opposed to working to end somebody else's oppression."[3] This kind of politics, the authors write, is called identity politics.

But, Barbara Smith explains, politics that are organized from within a collective identity aren't exclusionary. "We didn't mean that if you're not the same as us, you're nothing," she explains. "We were not saying that we didn't care about anyone who wasn't exactly like us. . . . It would be really boring only to do political work with people who are exactly like me."[4] The church has the potential to create space for negotiation, power analysis, solidarities, our failures to attend to them, and then our repentance after those failures. In baptism we come—in full recognition of ourselves and of our place within the hierarchies and histories our bodies bear—into the work of a renewed social order among us. The Combahee River Collective echoes back to me what I learn in the Gospels—that liberation does not erase ourselves but acknowledges the fullness of our lives and the political realities necessary for us to flourish.

Failure to attend to the bodies we bear, to the different work given to each of us, turns the good news into a strategy for quietism. A few years ago I heard a pastor offer up his church as a model for nonpartisan, apolitical worship. In his church, he bragged, ICE agents and undocumented people worship together and share the eucharist. I read this statement and wondered about the spiritual and emotional harm that occurs when we ask victims and their tormentors to be made one at the common meal of communion. What does it mean for us, as the body of Christ, to embody the unity of the Lord's supper with someone who, an hour later, could show up in uniform to kidnap someone from the same church, to disappear that person from the only life they know, to separate them from their family, friends, work, and community? I was not comforted by this thought. I was horrified.

It isn't enough to preserve Christian unity by maintaining the personal truth of each person in the congregation. When we offer communion, the sacrament of unity, to ICE agents and immigrant people without documentation, when we carve out an hour of worship in peace and then release people back into the world where the strong of the church will victimize the weak of the church, we make a choice. When we keep silent because politics is divisive and money is inflammatory, we make a choice. "'Washing one's hands' of the conflict between the powerful and powerless," writes Paulo Freire, "means to side with the powerful, not to be neutral."[5] We make this choice over and over again. This choosing is ongoing as we come up against new interrogations of ourselves, our communities, and our histories. The line between powerful and powerless shifts as we learn and discover more, as we face new questions, as we witness our neighbors in their struggles, and as we are called to the places we have not yet dared to go.

The Christian life is one where our unity is made known, is witnessed, in the working out of our theological lives. We sit beside the tombs of the world and wait for resurrection, knowing we await our own resurrection. Once on a Thursday in late

March, the New Jersey winds dropping the temperature dramatically, I pressed against a hundred people packed into an inconspicuous parking lot. I had had trouble finding the location, weaving between nondescript warehouses on the outskirts of an anonymous suburb. I had driven through fields of gray cinder block. Eventually I found the one I was looking for, number 20451. The white number on the building was the only sign that this warehouse didn't hold beams of wood or pallets of machinery like the others around it. It was a holding tank for people, a storage unit for humans.

I'd driven an hour from my home in Princeton to hold vigil for the undocumented people inside this private detention facility and to wash the feet of other people of faith. Inside the concrete building, immigrants awaited their fate. Some had crossed the ocean seeking asylum. Others were picked up by ICE. Each year a New Jersey advocacy group for immigrant justice organizes this vigil on Maundy Thursday, the day Jesus told his disciples to wash each other's feet.

We gathered to bring attention to the monetization of human life that happens in the private prison industry. These private prisons are all around us, but often out of sight and, their corporate managers hope, out of mind. But we also gathered because this is what it means to be one in Christ. We became a body. We sat on folding chairs, as a scratchy portable audio system read aloud an unintelligible liturgy we knew by heart. We knelt before one another, and we poured water over each other's feet with plastic jugs, pledging to continue working for the freedom of those who were just a few feet away on the other side of a concrete wall. The water from our feet wet the ground like tears.

Around us in the crowd were a few women, wives of some of the men who were in the detention center. We washed their feet, too, and we wept together before passing around a cold slice of pita bread, tearing off a round edge. "The body of Christ, for you," one of the women whispered in my ear. And then we dispersed, back into pickup trucks and minivans, back to homes and jobs, back to children without fathers, neighbors without neighbors, pieces of us left behind, pieces of us behind the heavy walls.

We wait beside tombs because this is where God shows up: where love leads us back to life without reason and often without hope. God appears in the places where there is nothing left but devastation, where there are only dead ends and solid walls, when no one is else coming. And it is here, waiting here where grief and terror break open, here that we discover the one who is there, calling us by name. Here we become one, and here Jesus makes himself known.

Kelly Brown Douglas re-narrates a stunning passage of Scripture when Jesus responds to those who look back on their lives only to realize they had overlooked the risen Jesus:

> "But lord, where did we see you dying and on the cross?" And Jesus would answer: "On a Florida sidewalk with Trayvon, or at the U.S./Mexican border with an immigrant refused asylum, or in a detention center with a brown child separated from his or her parents, or in a juvenile court with a black child trapped in the poverty-to-prison pipeline. As you did to one of the least of these, you did it me."[6]

We find Jesus murdered at the Pulse nightclub, Jesus with his neck under an officer's knees crying for his mama with his last breath, Jesus scrubbing racist graffiti from the side of a mosque. Our unifying belief in Jesus is a form our bodies take. In turn, Jesus is revealed in our collective body.

Without discerning, without knowing our histories and cultures and how our bodies and lives have been shaped by them, we are doomed to realign along the naturalized enmities Jesus calls us to dismantle. Jesus does not call us to claim we no longer have enemies. Instead, he shows us how to have enemies well. As Christians inhabit the body of Jesus, putting on Jesus like clothing (Romans 13:14), we take upon us those whom Jesus tells us are his life in the world. Their suffering is bound up in our lives. It becomes a part of our identity. When I confess that "it is no longer I who live, but it is Christ who lives in me" (Galatians 2:20), I confess that the men in the private immigration detention center are also a part of me. Their troubles are my troubles. Their enemies become my enemies.

As Jesus and then Paul follow the Holy Spirit's movement from the center of the covenant between God and Israel outward to the nations, as the work of God reorients all of creation around redemption, those who were formerly enemies are drawn into life together. Paul uses the metaphor of a body to describe the unity of the church in Corinth—diverse, unique parts that work together with Jesus as the operational center, the head (1 Corinthians 12). The unity of the church is not like a wartime truce or a bipartisan compromise. Paul doesn't use static, settled language to describe the church, because the church functions toward a particular end and purpose. The church acts toward the flourishing of creation. In the Bible we see the church formed when those who lived off the backs of the dispossessed become like those whose death was required for their thriving. They redistribute their money and reorient their social customs. They reject participation in economies of death and refuse to steal and kill for the empire.

Jesus himself speaks as a person formed within the long and terrible history of the occupation of Judea. Jesus inherits the threat of annihilation of the Jewish people. The challenge of the command to love your enemies and bless those who curse you (Matthew 5:44) is that Jesus assumes real violence, real degradation, real destruction. These are not misunderstandings. We love our enemies when we extend an invitation to a form of life where those who have the power to destroy others no longer exercise the self-destruction of hatred, hoarding, and violence. We love our enemies by creating a world that releases them from the wages of their own violence.

As it is, enmity is not a moral failure. Nor is it a feigned condition. It is the tangible expression of those who have experienced and witnessed horrific violence against them and their people. Kelly Brown Douglas writes about her experience of learning about this violence against Black people when she was a child:

> As a six or seven year old growing up in Dayton, Ohio, I heard the whispers of the adults around me talking about how awful it was that the church was bombed and how those four little girls were killed. I can remember hearing someone say that "the white man" who did it would probably never be caught, and if he were to be caught nothing was likely to happen to him.[7]

Douglas grew up watching on the nightly news as white police attacked children with dogs and turned firehoses onto protestors, tearing the skin from their bodies. She lived through the murder of Medgar Evers, walking up the driveway to his young family after work. These experiences cemented in her a particular understanding of the destructive power of whiteness.

Not all white people were out for Douglas's destruction. Yet she had every reason to believe white people were her enemies, bound up in active and passive participation in the torment of Black lives. Individual "good white people" are not enough to negate the experiences of Black terror. It is clear when I read Douglas's theology that she did not spend her life attempting to redeem white theology. Instead, she wrote theology from her identity as a Black woman. She invites others to learn the history of white supremacy in the church, in our white Jesus, to examine for ourselves the corruption of whiteness. Through her witness, people like me were able to meet Jesus, Black Jesus, rightly for the first time.

Our identity as Christians is interwoven into narratives of power. Because power is part of our lives, unity in the church is accompanied by disproportionate burdens. The burden of centrism is borne the most heavily by those who have the most to lose. Despite this, most often the people who stay and attempt to make change in the church are those without access to power. I have watched gifted women asked to shore up their energy to sit at the table with men in leadership who believe these women's calls to the pastorate are false or even an abomination. Black, Indigenous, and people of color are asked to take up the labor, often unpaid, of teaching their colleagues, neighbors, and churches about systemic racism, a system not of their own making that is not survivable for many people like them. Some queer people spend their lives working to be recognized as gifted and called leaders of the church.

People at the center of the dominant culture of power have little on the line in these negotiations. They can either be convinced to share power, or not. For everyone else, these experiences are costly, often a matter of life or death. People at the margins of power are asked to pull up a chair to a table designed for their exclusion. There is little choice in taking up this burden. Often their lives, and the lives of their people, depend upon it. For people with power—ecclesial, social, and economic —these are optional spaces with few consequences, regardless of their outcome.

To have enemies as a source of liberation—for ourselves and for those who do harm—is to recognize structures of power and their relationship to identity. The rest of this book explores how, through encounters with the Bible, Christians not only have enemies but have them well. We have enemies in particular and curious ways, ways that do not make sense within the structures of violent power-keeping around us. Instead, we are people who have set down our lives within the reconciliation of all things.

THREE

Praying for Enemies

NO GOOD COMES from our denial of enmity, and the Scriptures the church shares with Judaism testify to a form of prayer that announces the real, tangible threat of enemies. These prayers are offered by generations of people for whom God is their only refuge from death and despair. Psalms of lament are a cry for justice, witnessing to the terror of the world and God's refusal to desert the helpless.

Faye Brown was twenty-three when she went to prison. She died of COVID-19 in the North Carolina Correctional Institute for Women at the age of sixty-seven. Brown's is a textbook story of retributive justice and unfair sentencing. She was convicted after participating in a robbery to fund a drug habit. One of Brown's co-defendants killed a police officer who was pursuing the suspects. Despite no direct role in the death of the officer, in 1974 Brown was convicted of first-degree murder and sentenced with the death penalty. Her sentence was later commuted to life in prison.

Brown's case came to the North Carolina Supreme Court in 2009. Her lawyers argued that the Fair Sentencing Act deemed her punishment complete. Not only that, Brown was sorry. She'd changed. In prison she'd completed college and worked at a local cosmetology school. After thirty-five years in prison she was ready to contribute to the wider world.

Often during parole and resentencing hearings that involve the death of an officer, the courtroom crowds with police. Instead, at Brown's hearing the courtroom was packed with cosmetology students and clients who'd gotten to know Faye over the years. Despite this show of support, the local papers labeled her a cop killer, and none of the news reports carried details of the crime. The state claimed she was a violent menace to society, even though she'd never fired a weapon. During the robbery Brown had sat in the back seat of the car.

The courts rejected Faye Brown's case for completion of sentence. "Fundamentally it comes down to—is it retribution or is it rehabilitation? And I think that's the core of the debate," said Anita Earls, who then served as the Executive Director of the Southern Coalition for Social Justice.[1]

— — —

I STRAIN MY MEMORY for Brown, looking for her among the hundreds of women whose birthdays my church celebrates in the prison where she made her life. I think of her when we hold hands in a circle after birthday cake and charades, as she receives the blessing I say each time—"You are God's beloved, and that can never be taken from you." We anoint Miss Faye with oil in worship and sway with her to songs of praise and lament.

If she'd been released in 2010, if the state had accepted that her life should not be defined by those few terrible hours as a twenty-two-year-old, it's possible I would have met Brown on the outside. It's possible we could have been friends or sat beside each other in church. We might have worked together to welcome other women out of incarceration. Brown might have told her story of redemption, as she had to generations of women in prison who were desperate and afraid.

Instead, Brown succumbed to complications from COVID-19 after an outbreak in the prison system. For months prison advocates warned that social distancing is impossible in prisons, and as we'd seen in other places in the world, COVID-19 was spreading through prisons like wildfire. At the Butner prison, an hour north of the women's prison where Brown died, Juan Ledoux-Moreno, a seventy-four-year-old inmate serving one year for firearms and drug charges, died of complications due to coronavirus. He was scheduled for release in two months.

The virus coiled through our carceral system, entering through employees and work assignments, taking its toll among the inmate population. Despite warnings, calls, and advocacy work, the state continued to send the women of the North Carolina Correctional Institute for Women into government buildings on work assignments. They were earning one dollar a day to clean the buildings where they contracted coronavirus. Our congregation watched with panic and desperation as the women we knew and loved were infected.

These people were helpless from the grips of the disease and their deaths were unnecessary.

> By the rivers of Babylon –
>   there we sat down and there we wept
>   when we remembered Zion. (Psalm 137:1)

When I think of this terrible season of confinement and fear during the COVID-19 pandemic, my memory doesn't drift back to the goodness of the past, as it did for the exiled people of Israel, longing for their homeland. Instead, I weep into the long river of tears that ends here at the women's prison. It took centuries for this prison to take its current shape, decades to enact the laws that killed Faye Brown, and years more to convince us we are safer without Ms. Faye in our grocery stores, our churches, and our parks.

There are beautiful songs written to accompany the first lines of Psalm 137, haunting melodies about a lost and destitute people. That loss turns to prayer. All of the songs I know written from Psalm 137 end with the first verses. We might forget that the psalm continues, that it changes from rippling water to torrential rapids, threatening to drown anyone in its path. It ends with words of death for the future generations of Babylon's children:

> Remember, O Lord, against the Edomites
>   the day of Jerusalem's fall,
> how they said, 'Tear it down! Tear it down!
>   Down to its foundations!'
> O daughter Babylon, you devastator!
>   Happy shall they be who pay you back
>   what you have done to us!
> Happy shall they be who take your little ones
>   and dash them against the rock! (Psalm 137:7–9)

This level of rage stops me in my tracks, an unknowable anger, visceral and gleaming. It reminds us of the inseparability of grief and anger, and how rage can swell into the chaos of death and destruction.

I often remember the sermon the Reverend Jeremiah Wright preached on Psalm 137 the Sunday after the terrorist attacks of 9/11. In his sermon Wright reminded the people gathered for worship that they were likely familiar with this psalm but may not know its violent ending:

> Now in our class sessions on our church study trips, I have lifted up these verses to help our church members understand much of what it is they feel as they have stood in the slave castles in West Africa, as they have stood among the poverty in Ethiopia, stood in the townships of South Africa and stared at the favelas in Salvador da Bahia and Rio de Janeiro, in Brazil. African Americans have a surge of emotions as they see the color of poverty in the world of wealth and begin to understand that it is no accident that the world's poor are one color, and the world's rich are another color. When they tie together the pieces of five hundred years of colonialism, racism, and slavery with what they see in 2001, a surge of emotions hits them and the last three verses of Psalm 137 help them to understand what it is they are feeling.[2]

Wright told the congregation that the purpose of the psalm is not to report on God's action. It doesn't presume that God fulfills each person's cry for vengeance or even rescue, as if God were a conjuring trick that puts the world in order in the way people think it ought to be. The Psalms hold space, and often they hold space for lament. They give words to unspeakable suffering. They carve a vessel for unspeakable responses to this suffering.

The ancestors of our faith ask us to remember and reckon with violence and those who cause it. Wright, in this famous sermon, repeats the words: "the babies, the babies." What does it mean to enact revenge on the innocent? Making space for that kind of violence acknowledges the power of our unmitigated rage—violence for violence, destruction for destruction, terror visited upon generations.

Three weeks after Jeremiah Wright preached this sermon, after thousands lost their lives in the World Trade Center, as children were left without parents, after families and friends were ripped apart by the rising smoke and rubble of office buildings, the president of the United States, George W. Bush, dropped bombs on Afghanistan. That night a conflict began that grew like a weed, swelling from year to year and choking out hope for peace. Over the past two decades, the "war on terror" has killed over a million people, with millions more succumbing to illness and poverty and despair in refugee camps. Many were babies, children of the enemies of the United States.

— — —

THERE IS NO MISTAKING that the psalmist assumes the presence of enemies in the lives of those who love and serve the God of Israel. Page after page these prayers make room for vulnerable flesh and blood people to express the terror, danger, and trauma wrought by those who threaten and enact catastrophe. The most radical of these psalms are often labeled "imprecatory psalms." It's likely these psalms were set to the rhythm and structure of ancient curses. But imprecation is a misnomer. More than a curse, these psalms are movements of prayer that lament, that weep, and that wail over the calamity of lives, people, and futures. Each time, the writer releases from their hands the possibility of retributive violence and returns the action of justice back to God.

These psalms reach into the places of our fear and anxiety because they imagine terrible destruction on the enemies of the psalmist. This, along with the graphic nature of their descriptions (including the desire to see one's enemy shrivel up like a salted slug), led the lectionary compilers to excise these psalms from corporate worship. The Revised Common Lectionary, the rotation of Scriptures used by many churches in the world, cuts out the most troubling prayers expressed by the lament psalms. Several of these psalms were removed from the Liturgy of Hours, because the Roman Catholic Church deemed these verses an ethical deformation. For this reason it can be shocking for church people to discover that the Bible contains calls for intense judgment to be poured out upon the enemies of the writers.

These forceful and expressive psalms of lament are requests. In prayer people ask for God's anger to be tipped over like a pitcher of water onto their enemies. They pray for infliction of genital pain (Psalm 69:23), blindness (69:23), a rain of sulfur (11:6), the amputation of tongues and lips (12:3), and that their enemy's regular clothes be swapped out for "shame and dishonor" (109:29). Each time the psalmist speaks these words to God, they let go of their own participation in the destruction of their enemy, pushing the deepest wrath they can imagine into the hands of a holy judge.

The most breathtaking of these lament psalms imagines violence upon bystanders. The psalmists ask God to murder the children of their enemies and to cut off their future generations. Psalm 109 imagines false accusations being leveled at the writer. She imagines being on trial while an accuser asks a judge to have her spouse and children left widowed and orphaned, forced to beg for their survival on the streets. The psalmist seethes that her enemies wish infertility upon her, or the death of grandchildren—"name blotted out in the second generation" (109:13). As the writer looks at these stunning accusations, she turns the table back on her enemy: "May *that* be the reward of my accusers from the Lord" (109:20; italics added).[3]

Erich Zenger writes that the question about these psalms often comes to the church as "Do you really think that, as *Christians* (the question is never as *Jews* or as *human beings,* and certainly not as *victims of rape*) we can pray this way?"[4] In posing this question we overlook a truth of our world. People do cry out to God for vengeance because for some, at a certain point in suffering, it is impossible to see another way to bring an end to an unimaginable situation. These psalms preserve for our corporate memory the furthest extreme of human suffering. They are words that break open and pull water from the deepest well of anguish, from hell itself. If we chafe and cringe at these sulfurous prayers, it is, perhaps, because we have not lived teetering on the edge of last resort.

In the history of biblical interpretation, a popular form of dousing the heat of psalms of violence was to designate them as sinful, fallen expressions of human nature. C.S. Lewis described these psalms as wicked, devilish, sinful, and a "luxury of hatred."[5] This is the worst of us: our clawing thirst for the pain of others like blood on the page. Often Christians are taught that this vengeance is rectified in the life of Jesus, who reconciles enemies, becomes enmity himself, and makes reconciliation possible on the cross. Since we were enemies of God first, we are all reconciled under this grace. These psalms are relics of an old age and an old covenant.

Yet nowhere does Scripture condemn the psalter. In neither testament are these prayers upended or corrected. Instead, the

New Testament quotes from the psalms of God's vengeance.[6] In the gospel of John, Jesus enacts one of these psalms upon the economic engine of the temple, where coins inscribed with the face of Caesar were exchanged for temple money. As Jesus tears through the outer courtyard, turning over stalls and upsetting stacks of coins, his disciples remember the words of the psalmist, "Zeal for your house will consume me" (Psalm 69:9). The psalm continues:

> Let their table be a trap for them,
>   a snare for their allies.
> Let their eyes be darkened so that they cannot see,
>   and make their loins tremble continually.
> Pour out your indignation upon them,
>   and let your burning anger overtake them. (Psalm 69:22-24)

Jesus will quote this psalm again as a prophecy fulfilled—"They hated me without cause" (John 15:25). Jesus' body becomes this prayer against the system of economic exploitation on the edge of the temple. To be an enemy of Jesus is to be an enemy of God. Rather than dismissing the terror of the oppressed, Jesus puts his life in front of the flood of enemy destruction. Jesus bears the sorrows of the destitute in his body, allowing himself to be swept away into the drowning torrent of persecution by the wicked. These psalms are directed to God, and only God can answer these requests with direct action in the world, and so Jesus does.

— — —

I CANNOT IMAGINE wishing a stillbirth or genital mutilation on my worst enemy. But I also know the limits of my experience. I have enemies as an individual and in solidarity with communities pushed to the margins of power. Most of the lament psalms kept for us in the Bible are spoken from the internal life of someone who suffered grievous and—for me—unlived harm. These prayers preserve whispers and groans from the worst moments of someone's life. I do not know what it is like for someone to dig a pit and wait for my life to fall into it (Psalm 35:7). I do not know life-altering false accusations (Psalm 35:11), and I have not watched swords and arrows rip through the flesh of the poor (Psalm 37:14). People do not lie in wait, prowling like dogs, to tear me apart (Psalm 59:6). I do not know these experiences, but I bear witness.

One fall afternoon I disembarked from a small bus in the city of El Mozote in northeast El Salvador. Some of the houses on the town square were under construction that day as workers on scaffolding laid boards on an abandoned building. The sun was bright, and I could hear birds among purple wildflowers. A soft bundle of seeds clung to me by their bristles, and the ground was russet and green.

It was here that, during El Salvador's protracted civil war, soldiers massacred over one thousand women, children, and elderly villagers. Alma Guillermoprieto, a *Washington Post* reporter, fielded the story after she was escorted by soldiers into the small village in the territory of Morazán. She and another reporter, Robert Bonner, discovered the charred remains of children in rubble of adobe, a burned-out church, and layers of bodies beneath the decimated houses around the square. Skulls and spinal cords jutted through the burning ruins.

"By the end of the day," Guillermoprieto later reported, "I realized that something untoward and unspeakable had taken place."[7] The sole survivor, Rufina Amaya, made the massacre known to the public, how she hid herself in a tree while she listened to the screams of her community and her own children being slaughtered. The soldiers chose to strike when the men had gone to work in farms up the mountain, leaving behind the women, children, and elderly. Only the vulnerable would die at El Mozote.

Most of the people over fifty whom I met in El Salvador, including the tour guide of El Mozote, survived the conflict because they had fled to Guatemala to refugee camps. They were gone when hundreds of thousands of Indigenous people were murdered en masse around the country, but especially here in the north. The guide, a survivor of this village by chance—and now a memory keeper—recites the story of El Mozote, as I'm sure she has a hundred times. She points to a cardboard sign with grainy and aging pictures of the massacre, bones and earth in black and white, taken by a photographer for the *Washington Post*.

She then leads us to the place where the children were brought by soldiers to be slaughtered after their mothers were shot in the homes around the square. The soldiers needed to murder the mothers first; otherwise, the women would have been uncontrollable. The soldiers intuited that mothers will tear the world apart and overpower enemies if they see their children threatened.

At the center of the square is a tree, a tree I judged to be old by its thick trunk. I could see it in the photos surrounded by the still, charred remains of the massacre. Rufina Amaya is dead now, too, after spending her life telling others what happened to her children and her village. The tree remains to bear witness. I press my hand and think of the blood of the massacred that soaked into the roots. The blood of El Mozote runs in its limbs and leaves.

How can life go on here? I wondered. How does the ground not swallow up everything here and leave nothing behind? How does the grass not weep, the flowers not turn to stone? How can the site of this devastation give way to this ordinary life with another day of a builder working on a house and another day of children walking to school? "But life goes on," the guide tells me. Life goes on; remember El Mozote. *Presente*, El Mozote.

It is impossible to calculate this violence, to capture it. So I put my hand to the tree, let my palm scrape down the trunk to feel for a moment something like pain, a memory of burning in my skin. The psalms of revenging violence are like that, remembering the pain of the victims of El Mozote and of the Khmer Rouge, the echo of voices in Dachau, the weeping from children dying in isolation at the U.S.-Mexico border. In the psalms, I can run my hand down the gnarled trunk of remembrance, to take it into my body. This is what remains. Those who experienced these atrocities did not survive. But their voices survive and give voice to others. I am here to bear witness. I see, I remember, and I will tell.

— — —

I'VE HEARD CHRISTIANS confront the ethical question of the psalms of vengeance. They worry over the ill that could come if these words are prayed from our pulpits and in our private prayers. They fear what could happen with the expression of our rage. My concern moves in the opposite direction. I fear the cool and collected roadmap of civility that denies those who have experienced trauma the space for public expression of that anger, which lingers in the air as palpable discomfort for the powerful.

I have seen my city council call down decorum rules on a Black mother who erupted at a public meeting over the death

of her Black child at the hands of police. I've watched elected officials chastise the methods of protestors after decades of
unresponsiveness to impacted community members' pleading
through peaceful protests, letter writing, and public comment.
I've watched queer people reprimanded for interrupting business as usual, despite decades of silencing them through resolu-
tions, Robert's Rules of Order, and by-laws. People who occupy
seats of power control the agenda by censuring the anger of
those demanding change. Certain voices, "respectable" voices,
are given space while others are shut out.

The psalms that call for God's intervention are written as a
reminder of the enormity of human suffering within systemic
and sustained forms of violence that cannot always be rectified
by good work, good intentions, or reasonable dialogue. They
show us the way that power is structured across and within interpersonal relationships and geopolitical realities. Rather than
showing resignation or reasonableness, the psalms keep before
us the trauma of inequitable suffering. These psalms hold the
space, and they push us all toward response.

In psalms of justice we hear the cry of those whose words
mark the places of oppression and degradation in history. These
are people who are acted upon, who apprehend their own help-
lessness before coiling, suffocating violence. These are people
whose very existence hangs in the balance of political and economic forces beyond their control. There will be no negotiation or discussion, nothing to bargain with, no scheme, no
outsmarting, no escape. These are the prayers of dead-ends.

And yet something else happens here. To speak this violence aloud is also to generate a hope which destruction cannot overcome. To make space for the words of those facing
catastrophe, who have nowhere left to turn, who have nothing

left—this is the memory preserved in the psalms. "In the face of monstrous evil, the worst thing is not to express anger," writes J. Clinton McCann, "it is to feel nothing. What must be felt is grief, rage, and outrage. In their absence, evil becomes an acceptable commonplace. To forget is to submit to evil, to wither and die; to remember is to resist, be faithful, live again."[8] The psalms of rage remind us that somehow, in spite of absolute defeat, someone dared to say aloud that the world is not as it should be.

In my own prayer I sense no conflict between the psalms of justice and the New Testament's call to love our neighbors as the way to describe prayer for our persecutors. The prayers offered in the Bible include those by Zechariah, asking God to save us from the hands of all who hate us. The prayers of the Gospels encompass Mary's Song, a call to tear the powerful from their thrones and send the rich away empty. Throughout his ministry Jesus is intolerant of prayers meant to look pious. He lashes out at prayers being used as a public gesture rather than as an offering to God of one's internal orientation. I would guess that praying as we "ought to pray" falls in line with the false piety of those who pray loudly on the street corners so that "they may be seen and praised by others" (Matthew 6:2).

Jesus gives a rough outline of how to pray in light of this remarkable change of perspective. We start by positioning our prayer from the place where God is in control of history, working things out in the world around us, not distant from it. God is charged with the care of creation. We can let go of outcomes, of our attempts to control history. "Our Father in heaven. Your name is holy." We recognize that God's kingdom is established, firmed up in our midst. Our desires, our intentions for the righting of wrong, the reign of justice—let it come to pass.

After we have established God's reign, Jesus tells us to offer our own needs. In this prayer, Matthew slips out of Hebrew, the formal language of the Temple, and into Aramaic, the everyday language of the people. It is in this language in which people argued in the market and whispered to their children as they went to sleep. The purpose of prayer is to move ordinary life and common speech into the communal form of God's reign.

I suspect Jesus uses this informal language because there is no point in offering up prayers about the things we ought to want. Prayer may be transformative of our desires, but it will not be so by pretending we are something we are not. Rather than putting out pious prayers for public consumption or pretending that God doesn't already know what we desire, we come to God as we are. Herbert McCabe reminds us that "genuine prayer means honest prayer, laying before your Father in heaven the actual desires of your heart—never mind how childish they may sound. Your Father knows how to cope with that."[9] We pray for the things we want and the things we need because we can't fool God. In the end, we only fool ourselves.

"One of the great human values of prayer is that you face the facts about yourself and admit to what you want," McCabe tells us, "and you know you can talk about this to God because he is totally loving and accepting."[10] This is why Jesus tells his followers to stop babbling like the pagans. This kind of prayer is an extraction exercise; stone and wood idols are impersonal amulets that intercede to reckless deities. The prayer Jesus offers to us makes space to come face-to-face with who we are and to deal with it plainly, alongside someone who loves us absolutely and unconditionally.

I have offered forthright prayers, prayers asking God to remove, by any means necessary, the leader of my country. I have asked God to cause buildings to crumble and people to lose their jobs. I prayed these prayers in honesty, placing my anger before a holy God. And more often than not my prayers were not misplaced in their earnestness and longing for a world set right. At other times, my prayers of wrath, seething with demands for punishment and revenge, revealed that my own incoherent and blistering rage would do nothing to set me and others down in the renewed order of God's creation. What I really wanted was pain. In these prayers, I reengaged the cyclical violence of perpetual struggle, only now on behalf of victims. But until I said the words aloud, until it was held before me, I could not see another way out.

‒ ‒ ‒

AS IT IS, there are times we pray the prayer of vengeful justice for ourselves. At other times our prayers are acts of solidarity. We pray as witness, as a steadfast refusal to let the voices of those who have been tortured, murdered, abused, and raped fall silent. At the border of Douglas, Arizona, and Agua Prieta, Mexico, a group of people gather for the weekly Healing Our Borders prayer vigil. At dusk, with traffic backed up at the port of entry, participants form a line on the sidewalk. A handcart passes by, filled with white crosses. Some of the small crosses carry names. Others say Mother, Sister, Friend, or Husband. Each cross represents a person who died in the Sulphur Springs Valley attempting to cross to a new life in the United States.

This isolated stretch of desert was once quiet and empty. But as Mark Adams, one of the vigil's organizers, explains, due to the "prevention through deterrence" border policy of the Clinton administration, along with the economic upturn of the 1990s and the devastation of the Mexican economy as a result of free trade agreements, it is now a popular crossing for migrants. U.S. policy pushed people away from safe places of crossing and into these deadly areas. "Our policy is intentionally lethal."[11] We legislate for death.

The long row of people with crosses sweeps down the sidewalk outside the official port of entry where cars drive in and out of Mexico and the United States. One by one we each stop, holding our crosses aloft as we say the name or identity scrawled in marker. We shout, "Presente!"—"Here." Our nation's murdered are present among us.

Some of the migrants were killed by border crossing decades ago, the date of their death inscribed on each cross. In the calculation of the government, these lives are worthless. They will be forgotten, a necessary sacrifice to the ever-expanding economy of the United States. But each week a Catholic priest and a Presbyterian pastor refuse to let their lives be forgotten.

As the wagon empties I see the street lined with over a hundred crosses. Each represents a person made in God's image who died in the valley. After Pastor Mark gathers us in a circle, he offers a prayer, then stands in the middle of our human ring. "Presente!" he shouts without warning, hands cupped to his mouth. I am startled by the sound after the quiet of the prayer. Turning to the south he shouts the word again. "Presente!" He shouts the word in each direction—north, south, east, and west. It is the final prayer. There is fire in the air.

FOUR

Shared Anger and Forgiveness

ANGER IN THE PSALMS offers clarity about the danger and terror in the world and illuminates how this danger and terror arrives in our congregations and communities. When we welcome this anger's presence, rather than tamping down its energy, we find the power to create a community of resistance, and that makes forgiveness a possibility. "Anger denied subverts community," writes Beverly Harrison; without anger we run the risk of falling into passive aggression or moralizing self-righteousness. "Anger expressed directly is a mode of taking the other seriously, of caring," Harrison goes on. She places anger within the work of love.[1] When anger takes form in communal sharing, it can carve the path toward reconciliation.

I do not often hear of churches working toward cultivating shared anger. I suspect that many of our churches are in the habit of avoiding expressions of anger and keeping conflict at bay. Anger is dangerous and divisive. But without making space for anger, the church cannot offer safe harbor to people who are suffering at the hands of others. When we cultivate communal anger, we create communities that share burdens and creatively enact justice.

Willie Jennings writes that the discipline of hope in this racial world, "in this white supremacist-infested country called the United States of America, requires anger." This is not anger that must be converted to peace, as if anger is the inverse of peace. Instead, Jennings writes, "This anger, my anger, is connected to the righteous indignation of God." He confesses that there is "great danger and great power" in drawing the connection between God's anger and our anger. We can identify this connection when we ascertain certain characteristics. One is that our anger must be shareable. It is not enough for those who encounter the suffering of others, of racial violence, to say, "I can't imagine what you are feeling."[2] Instead, Jennings writes,

> One of the most stubborn barriers to overcoming this racial world is the refusal of so many people to take hold of black anger. It is a particular sickness of whiteness that invites people to imagine themselves as spectators of racial suffering and observers of black pain who are allowed to feel only assorted forms of white guilt.[3]

In the church committed to gathering around shared anger, we affirm that "God wants us to hate what God hates. God invites us into a shared fury, but only the kind that we creatures can handle."[4] Communities of reconciliation can emerge out of this anger by identifying a common enemy. And only in this identification can we begin to tell the truth about the need for that enemy to relent of their violence and to join the work of God.

In communities of shared anger we discover lingering within us our own participation in the destruction of others. Anger, like a fire, can offer light which illuminates the forms of destruction that are active within our own lives and communities. If we don't individually and collectively confront the enemy we inhabit, we are doomed to displace responsibility onto others. Because the church is a community of reconciliation, we recognize that we bear both victim and victimizer in our bodies. The work of truth-telling about our enemies is not simply to identify who is against us "out there," but to help us lay down our enmities toward one another within the complicated terrain of our lives, our relationships, our multiple and intersecting identities, and our action in the world.

When anger binds us together, revealing and burning away, it becomes holy. In 1972, the brutal Park Chung Hee regime came to power in Korea through a military coup. Park's legacy is mired with hired hit men and secret police who crushed opposition and assured Park's rule. The regime tortured dissidents with such ferocity that they claimed they could manage any change of heart short of "turning men into women or women into men."[5]

Throughout this time ordinary people in Korea, including students and workers, protested the suspension of democracy in the Yushin Constitution. Those who opposed Park's rule faced brutal oppression through arrest, torture, and execution.[6] The Association of the Families of the Arrested (Kukahyup) formed around the outrage and grief that welled up from the space left by murdered and disappeared family members. In the midst of this terror and repression, this group of Christian women gathered for Thursday night prayer meetings. Their gatherings bristled with rage. Mothers wept and screamed, "Throw away the murderous regime."[7]

The women's shared anger led to the creation of structured burden-sharing. In his interviews with the women of Kukahyup, Wonchul Shin discovered a social network, *pumashi*, that organized the women's resistance. *Pumashi* is traditionally a Korean agricultural system of labor sharing. In the hands of the women, it was repurposed to describe an interpersonal mode of resistance in which the women supported one another and attended each other's trials.[8] Their anger, far from destructive, provided the fuel to enact the good that had been denied them by the terror of the Park regime.

Anger does not dissipate when denied. It festers or it explodes, because anger is charged with power. For the women of Kukahyup, prayer meetings were a place to give that anger to others who were experiencing the same disaster. "They shared their burdens of anger with one another, and their shared burdens enabled them to achieve their own flourishing, the affirmation and embrace of life, not the destructive consumption and sacrifice of life."[9] Their anger created a community of resistance. In destitution, they carved out a form of life that demanded justice.

— — —

OUR FEARS ABOUT ANGER, about its potential for destruction, are held within the life of Jesus. Jesus pushes our anger back from the edge of hatred, from going over the cliff of unshared, unexamined destruction. Instead of turning away from anger, we are invited to "step into it and into God's own righteous indignation."[10] Uniting ourselves to God's anger is the force that drives us toward one another and toward the hopeful possibility of a new world.

In the New Testament Jesus is angry. He expresses frustration with his disciples, condemns leaders of his own tradition, and curses a fig tree in irritation. At the same time, Jesus offers a stunning teaching against anger:

> "You have heard that it was said to those of ancient times, 'You shall not murder'; and 'whoever murders shall be liable to judgment.' But I say to you that if you are angry with a brother or sister, you will be liable to judgment." (Matthew 5:21-22a)

This teaching about anger follows the beatitudes. In this section of the Sermon on the Mount, Jesus instructs the beloved community about the peculiar character they will take up in the world. Here we learn that unexamined, individually borne anger can be a force that propels us toward murderous destruction. Or we can cultivate communal anger that leads us away from sin (Ephesians 4:26).

Jesus' words shape a form of communal life. How we approach this life within the community of God, according to Jesus, takes a different form because it no longer relies on the same hierarchical structures of violence that secure the old order. We within the church hold anger in a particular way. In the old order, anger ends in discipline and rejection because it is bound to powers and principalities that repress and destroy. By contrast, the beloved community is a vessel within which it is possible for anger to be reimagined toward the wholeness of all.

We see this at work as Jesus cautions those of the beatified community to work out their concerns with one another rather than relying on a judicial system which substitutes retribution for reparation as a simulacrum for justice (Matthew 5:25-26). Anger acts as a signal to draw attention to a harm or a wrong. When we see it this way, as the response when a harm or wrong remains unrectified, then we have moved from anger as a threat to anger as potential.

Audre Lorde writes about the power of this kind of anger. "My fear of anger taught me nothing," she told a group of women gathered for the National Women's Studies Association Conference. "Your fear of that anger will teach you nothing, also."[11] Anger was Lorde's correct and accurate response to racism. The purpose of that anger was not to elicit guilt and defensiveness. Anger that elicits this kind of response is no more than "bricks in a wall against which we all flounder."[12] Instead, Lorde allowed the fears her anger inspired in others to offer "spotlights" that could search out the possibility of mutual growth.

Lorde talks about her experiences of being Black and a woman in the world, sharing with other Black women "who live and survive thousands" of racist encounters, often asked to reduce their bodies, their voices, and their anger for the sake of white women's comfort. Often women, but especially Black women, question the way their rage emerges "as useless and disruptive."[13] Lorde offers a different way of engaging anger:

> Every woman has a well-stocked arsenal of anger potentially useful against those oppressions, personal and institutional, which brought that anger into being. Focused with precision, it can become a powerful source of energy, serving progress and change.... I am speaking of the basic and radical alteration in those assumptions underlining our lives.[14]

Anger offers potential strength and clarification for the work before us.

Lorde speaks about a space that I hope the church can also cultivate: a space of shared and refined anger as a form of clarification, "For it is in the painful process of this translation that we identify who are our allies with whom we have grave differences, and who are our genuine enemies."[15] One of the challenges for the church is creating space for difference while at the same time discerning when this difference takes on forms of power that make a turn toward enmity. Anger is the clarifying force that helps us to make the distinction.

The communal life of the church, at its best, does not hold a center of limitless, tolerable difference. It makes space for those "grave differences," while recognizing that there are both tolerable and intolerable differences. The shift from difference to enmity is bound up in power—who has access to it and who does not, and how it is used against some for the flourishing of others.

Thomas Aquinas offers a warning through the words of John Chrysostom: "Unreasonable patience is the hotbed of many vices, it fosters negligence, and incites not only the wicked but even the good to do wrong."[16] If we lack anger at injustice, we are unable to rightly discern and act in the world. Anger is the source of energy that aids the discovery of our common task, both as a forum to convey information and to help us burn through the chaff to reveal the source of our discontent.

— — —

IN THE CHURCH we discover how to be angry about the same concerns and then how to bear that anger together as a creative force to build something new. To be clear—I do not want the call to discern what angers God to devolve into checklists of difficult or controversial topics, then figuring out a joint position, from abortion to where we ethically shop for groceries. A legalistic approach to shaping our common life would be catastrophic. Instead, the church makes space to work out ways of being in which anger emerges as a force not of destruction but of scorching clarification. Our discovery is possible because we dwell in the life of God. And in this life, we are bound up in forgiveness.

A chapter on anger may seem like a strange place to talk about forgiveness, but only if we conceive of forgiveness as happening only after human relations have fallen apart. One theological school conceives of forgiveness in this way—as "plan B," in which forgiveness is God's reaction in the wake of our human failure. In this way of conceiving human brokenness, the rifts in our human community reflect the original sin in the Garden of Eden. After Adam and Eve break apart creation's potential for eternal harmony, Jesus is sent by God to offer a fix.

But there is another way to understand Jesus' place in the story of salvation. Instead of a rescue effort, Jesus offers forgiveness as the first order, the form of life that binds us to Jesus as God's embodied reign of peace. If we are to imagine God becoming flesh in Jesus in this way, it is not because the first attempt at perfection failed. Instead, Jesus, "slain from the foundation of the world" (Revelation 13:8 KJV), comes to us as the incarnation, independent of sin. "God brings creatures into being, or, to put it still more sharply, creation happens because God wills to take flesh," writes Ian McFarland, "and God cannot do that without bringing into being the world that flesh inhabits."[17] Before sin, before people, before stars, before the formless void, Jesus was there, outside of time, working and willing a reconciled creation into being.

In the church people form their lives within the reconciliation of the crucified Jesus, the Son of God, who absorbs the
enmity of the world into the cross and renews creation. Jesus
comes to us not grudgingly but because God wills to share the
divine life with us. As it is, forgiveness is the form that life takes
for people who are united to Christ. This does not protect us
from conflict or division, neither does it stop us from giving
and receiving harm. But within this life, in-dwelling within the
renewed order of creation, we are forged of God's forgiveness.

Jesus gets to the heart of this forgiveness in a parable in
Matthew 18. How many times, Peter asks, must he forgive?
Jesus answers by telling the disciples a story: "The reign of God
can be compared to a king who wished to settle accounts with
his slaves" (Matthew 18:23). The king in Judea at the time this
parable was preserved in writing is not a good and compas-
sionate sovereign. Whatever Jesus says next will be tinged with
the reputation of the hot-blooded, mean-tempered, murderous
rulers of the Roman Empire.

To our surprise this leader quickly changes directions from
the expected outcome. In the story a contract has been broken
and a debt accrued that cannot be paid off. A slave owes a king
ten thousand talents, an unseemly amount of money. It is more
than a person could repay another. The man in debt wants a
way out. To follow the logic of debt to repayment would end
his life. And so he begs for a new way. Instead of reducing the
terms by turning out a payment plan or offering the option of
collateral on the debt, the king cancels the debt altogether.

This is a messianic act of forgiveness. The master gives the
slave back his life. Everything is on the line—his wife, his children, his possessions. Once a subject of the old order—to the
economics of dispossession, of the sale of human bodies, to

hierarchies and debts—the ruler offers the slave a way out. The king has compassion, the same compassion that Jesus shows when he stumbles upon the political refugees in the wilderness and heals them and feeds them (Matthew 9:36).

Peter, no doubt, hoped for this ending. In his vision the messiah would come to change the system from the top. God's redemption would prevail by dethroning the tyrants of Rome and installing the messianic reign. Certain servants would receive their just reward of forgiveness and honor. In Peter's mind, and for the rest of the disciples, this would be where the parable ends. But as Peter walks away, Jesus pulls him back. There is more.

Trickle down justice doesn't have its intended effect. In an identical scene, Jesus describes how the ruler's model of forgiveness does little to sway the future actions of the first slave. A second slave also has a debt that he can't repay. This time the debt is owed to the first slave, and, again, the one owing a debt begs for a way out. He wants out of the whole system. He wants forgiveness. Instead, we learn that the first servant reverts back to the old logic. He wants what is due him by right. And he throws the man into debtor's prison to work until he can pay off the debt.

What happens next is shocking. The king who forgave the unforgiveable debt hears reports about what has happened, and he goes to find the first servant. He says, "You wicked slave! I forgave you all that debt because you pleaded with me. Should you not have had mercy on your fellow slave, as I had mercy on you?" (Matthew 18: 32-33). Then the king throws this slave out. He hands him over to torturers who will force him to repay everything he owes.

I can guess we're a bit on edge about this story because the person identified as the king is God. The discomfort I sense at this ending is matched by people who sense a different kind of terror in this story, a trauma that emerges from being victims. This parable is often a burden for those who hear in it that they must forgive their abusers and oppressors. Stories of required forgiveness are painful for people who are not ready to forgive those who have assaulted or harmed them. There are churches who harbor abusers for decades because of Jesus' radical teaching on forgiveness, each time assumedly excusing behavior in favor of forgiveness, seventy times seven.

This is why it is significant that the ending, despite its discomfort, releases us from a contractual form of forgiveness that only serves to recapitulate systems of destruction for those who have been harmed. The first servant is handed over to authorities who demand as he demands, who order the world as he has ordered it.

The first slave refused to function within the order of his master, according to the logic and economy of his kingdom—of forgiveness. When it becomes clear that this slave would not return the same act of forgiveness, instead reverting to the terror of an old order situated on fairness and getting what you deserve, God hands him over to it. When Matthew says "gives him over" he is using the language of transferring someone, turning them over to the power of another.

The metaphor in this parable runs the length of the New Testament. We are told that we choose whose world we want to live in. We'll choose wealth or God. We'll choose violence or God. We'll choose nationalism or God. We'll choose racial hierarchy or God. Each case is an example of a different and incompatible operational system. One of those systems, if we live by it, binds us in endless struggle and violence that leads to our own destruction, as well as the destruction of others.

If we balk at God's anger in this story, it may be because we have eliminated the possibility of a God who willingly releases us back to the old order to which we have pledged allegiance. In the Bible we discover that there is room for both compassion and anger in God. God is angry when people use forgiveness to justify hiding predators, overlooking the suffering of their victims. God is angry when we fall back on the old order of punishment and repayment of debt. To unite ourselves to Jesus is to rest into the grace of the renewed order of creation. Mutual destruction awaits us in the old order.

From this parable we learn the considerable harm that occurs when we continue, corporately or individually, to expect forgiveness without extending it, without mutuality and reciprocity among a people who are entrenched in forgiveness. It is no surprise, then, that the teaching that precedes the story of the slave who is unwilling to forgive a debt is the teaching about how the church discerns its life together and attends to harm:

> If a member of the church sins against you, go and point out the fault when the two of you are alone. If the member listens to you, you have regained that one. But if you are not listened to, take one or two others along with you, so that every word may be confirmed by the evidence of two or three witnesses. If the member refuses to listen to them, tell it to the church; and if the offender refuses to listen even to the church, let such a one be to you as a Gentile and a tax collector. (Matthew 18:15-17)

If the person who has caused harm—the abuser and the victimizer—won't accept what they've done and make it right, they are to be treated as a tax collector or a Gentile.

Jesus does not offer up these two examples because Gentiles and tax collectors are ethically worse than Jews or have no place in God's kingdom. He doesn't give this as an example of people to be shunned or hated or ridiculed. Tax collectors and Gentiles were a regular facet of Jewish society. Jesus visits the home of tax collectors. Throughout Jesus' ministry we meet Gentiles who come to believe, who are healed, and who bear witness to the overflow of the kingdom of God out from Israel and into the world. Tax collectors and Gentiles are mentioned in this story of shaping church accountability because they operate within a different logic than that of Jesus. They operate outside a way of life shaped by God's covenantal love. Their commitments, the way they order their world, isn't compatible with the new order that Jesus initiates.

That old order, represented by Gentiles and tax collectors, prescribes vengeance as punishment. In the economics of the pagan world, relationships are useful for getting ahead as people climb the social ladder. The people who matter are those with access to money and political power. Jesus upsets this way of organizing social and religious life. The logic of Gentiles and tax collectors is incompatible with the reign of God. To treat people in the church who refuse to follow the path of accountable, holistic reconciliation like Gentiles and tax collectors is not to hate these people or to seek revenge or punishment. Instead, we are to treat those who have chosen to operate outside of the order of God's redeeming love with caution and hope of their return, but without continuing to subject ourselves to their harm.

We are asked to choose which world we want to live in—a world of retributive justice or a world of forgiveness. Karl Barth, reflecting on forgiveness, writes, "Living by forgiveness is never by any means passivity, but Christian living in full activity."[18] Barth writes that, when we finally come before God, we will not be asked to give an account of our piety or morality. Instead, we will be asked, "Did you live by grace, or did you set up gods for yourself and perhaps want to become one yourself?"[19]

We can't operate in both orders. And when the world of revenge enters the renewed creation, the order built on good news, it poisons the possibility of mutuality, transformation, and reconciliation. The way out of the endless loop of retribution is to recognize that forgiveness of individuals is interwoven with the social order of God's reign. Transformative justice offers practices that realize this in communities broken by violence. In transformative justice, interpersonal reconciliation provides individual accountability for harm without isolation or punishment. In this model "individual justice and collective liberation are equally important, mutually supportive, and fundamentally intertwined."[20] To realize one is to realize the other.

The movement toward transformative justice emerged through people who desired community accountability without turning to police or prisons to have that justice realized. For this kind of accountability to take shape, we first recognize that we emerge into a world shaped by violence—from top to bottom. "Violence is collectively enabled," writes Mia Mingus, "has a collective impact and requires a collective response."[21] The process of healing from harm, getting to the source of our anger, requires attention to the conditions that make harm possible.

Ejeris Dixon writes that one of the first question of transformative justice is, "What is the world we want?"[22] Both holy anger and righteous forgiveness find their source in this question.

What is the world we want? When we begin here our conflicts and their endings open us to new possibilities, taking us out of the frameworks of retribution and punishment, and into transformation and healing.

FIVE

Mary's Politics

SHARED ANGER IS A TOOL that shapes and refines collectives. Through the burden-sharing of anger, these communities of ordinary people become powerful in the face of destructive forces. We witness this in the New Testament, where communities of the dispossessed are transformed into harbingers of the good news, the announcement that God is toppling the enemies of sin and death. For centuries women laid the groundwork for this kind of collective political solidarity. In their lives we see how resistance to enemies is born from refusal to accept the terms handed down by the powerful. Many times these groups of women pattern themselves after prophets like Mary who announce in their lives that Jesus is for the dispossessed. In life, as in the Scriptures, enemies are overcome not through tolerance but by making the world new.

The gospel of Luke makes clear what is it at stake for the people of God against the enemies of the state. The gospel identifies by name those who will attempt to crush Jesus, among them the archetypal Roman enemies: Herod the Great and his son, Herod Antipas. Herod Antipas is tetrarch of Galilee and a remnant of the Hasmonean dynasty. A brooding storm hangs over every scene in Luke where Herod is present, and it portends lightning ready to strike. Halfway through the gospel, the reckless and tyrannical Herod reaches new heights of evil with the shocking beheading of John the Baptist.

Not long after, sensing the growing threat to Jesus, "Pharisees came and said to him, 'Get away from here, for Herod wants to kill you'" (Luke 13:31). Jesus replies saying, "Go and tell that fox for me, 'Listen, I am casting out demons and performing cures today and tomorrow, and on the third day I finish my work'" (Luke 13:32). Jesus travels to Jerusalem, to the city where prophets are murdered. He comes to die. This exchange not only relays the complex relationship Jesus has to the Pharisees (here, as a group who want to warn him away from danger) but also the way Jesus inflames tensions by hurling the insult of "fox" at Herod.

I'd heard the adage "fox in the henhouse," but it came to life when I visited a friend who kept chickens on their sprawling acreage. As we watched her cheerful hens strut through the grass, she described for me the eerie silence that greeted her one autumn morning as she went to collect eggs. When she reached the coop she saw a small hole in the door where the wire had been pried back. Then her eyes turned toward the ground, covered with feathers and blood. "It was gruesome," she told me. "You don't realize how much damage one fox can do." I imagined similar scenes of carnage that Herod "the fox" enacted on the people of Judea.

Up to this point in Luke's gospel, Herod has shown little rancor toward Jesus. Instead, he appears genuinely curious about this new prophet. Matthew's gospel includes an episode with the father of Antipas, Herod the Great, querying the magi about the location of Jesus' birth and slaughtering the newborn Hebrew babies. But this early threat is absent from Luke. Instead, an uncomfortable silence greets us as Herod slowly begins to piece together the danger of Jesus. We sense a shift in the narrative. The fox, having murdered Jesus' predecessor, John the Baptist, seeks new prey.

Prophets are killed in Jerusalem, Jesus tells the astonished crowd. What more is to be expected for me?

Several writings from around the same period as Luke's gospel give us a better idea of the force of the insult that Jesus casts on Herod. Epictetus's *Discourses* contains a description of the various animals that occupy ancient Roman society:

> Some of us incline to become like wolves, faithless and treacherous and mischievous: some become like lions, savage and bestial and untamed; but the greater part of us become foxes and other worse animals. For what else is a slanderer and a malignant man than a fox, or some other more wretched and meaner animal?[1]

Operating within this cultural context, Jesus groups Herod with the despicable fox.

We also discover something of Herod's character in the Mishnah, a collection of Jewish stories and teachings from the first century. In one story, rabbis discuss a recent governmental ban on gathering to study the Bible. When one rabbi asks Rabbi Akiva if he isn't afraid of disobeying the command, he responds with this story: once a fox was walking along the riverbank and saw fish in the water swimming from one place to another. The fox said to the fish, "From what are you fleeing?" The fish replied, "The nets of men." The fox then suggested, "Why not come out of the water to live with me, as my ancestors once lived with your ancestors?" To this the fish said, "Aren't you the one they call the cleverest of animals? You are not clever but foolish. If we live now in a place that causes fear, how much more in the element in which we would die!" A fox is an enemy lying in wait, ready to destroy both body and soul.[2]

There is no doubt that Herod knew these characterizations of the fox. Being labeled a fox would no doubt send him into a rage. Herod, a Roman ruler, would want to be compared to an eagle, the symbol of Rome. Instead, he is lumped in with a malicious fox, who jockeys for power but is ultimately revealed as impotent and reviled. Instead of power and influence, the fox brings devastation—destruction of the workers in God's vineyard. John Darr calls Herod the Fox "a would-be disrupter of God's divine economy."[3] Herod is a predator in the worst way, the kind that is a deadly, yet unworthy, opponent.

- - -

IN THE DISRUPTIVE REIGN of God, the foil to Herod is not the eagle with its armies and kings. It is a teenager, pregnant outside of marriage, a poor girl from a backwater town on the outskirts of the capital city. She is the wretched of the Earth, and within her body is the one who will end the power of the Herods of this world for good.

This woman, Mary, the mother of God, appeared to Juan Diego, a Mexican peasant, for the final time in a series of visions, on December 12, 1531. Mary's first appearance to Juan came several days earlier. After the visitation, the boy ran to tell the bishop, who would not believe that the mother of God would bother with an uneducated peasant. At her next appearance, Juan requested a sign from the Lady, and she agreed to meet him at a certain place and time.

By the next day Juan's sick uncle was nearing death, and Juan was sent to fetch a priest for a final confession. In doing so he missed his appointment with Mary. Late and exasperated, Juan hurried to the place they had agreed to meet. Along the way the boy found the Virgin Mary waiting for him. *¿No estoy yo aquí que soy tu madre?* she said. "Am I not here, I who am your mother?" Juan went home to find his uncle miraculously healed, the sign he had requested.

The artist Carole Taylor created life-sized icons of four varieties of Mary, each from a different culture. The icons invite participants to explore the universality and particularity of Jesus' mother as she appears in a variety of cultures around the world. Taylor's art allows us to see Mary as different yet the same—Our Mother—in altered clothing, a common body with skin the color of the people whom she visits, her voice a comforting solidarity, speaking the language of common people: Quechua, Japanese, Italian, or Cheyenne.

Taylor's Marys are life-sized paper dolls made of industrial cardboard and painted with acrylic. Each wears the clothing of the culture in which she appeared. Taylor made these outer garments interchangeable. When I saw the Marys they stood like four church greeters, or perhaps sentinels, waiting for me—Juan Diego's Virgin of Guadalupe alongside Our Lady of Lourdes, the Byzantine Theotokos, and Madonna and Child of Soweto. The paper dolls reminded me that Mary comes to ordinary people, speaking their language and giving them hope.

Mary is often neglected in the religious life of Protestants and Anabaptists, a casualty of our painful separation from the

Roman Catholic Church. Yet Mary awaits our attention in Scripture. Against the backdrop of Herod's tyranny and terror, Luke's gospel preserves Mary's prophecy about enemies in a song. She is the mother of all those like Juan Diego, people under the sword of Herod, those who are not believed, who face the knife and the gun, and who are threatened with exile and hunger.

The reign of God begins in the body of Mary. The first announcement of what the kingdom looks like, what will happen, who it will topple—it begins here with Mary's song. She is the first to proclaim the gospel. My friend Isaac Villegas likes to say that Jesus learned how the reign of God would look from his mother, as the words that had been passed down to Mary from the angel Gabriel were whispered into Jesus' ear, sung to him each night as a lullaby.[4] The turning of tables, the woe to the righteous, the call to the rich young man to sell all he has—this is prophesied at the beginning and taught to Jesus as he grows.

Mary is the first priest, the first to offer Jesus' body to the world. She nurtures that body, teaches him, feeds him from her breast, and tells him the story of Israel's enemies, of deliverance from slavery in Egypt, too. She teaches him the prophets and the plagues, of the cloud by day and the fire by night. In the gospel of Luke, Mary sings words of liberation to her cousin Elizabeth. Hers are words of liberation from enemies, from the likes of Herod and from all the foxes of the world. The occasion is Elizabeth's blessing on Mary and the baby she holds in her womb. Elizabeth is the first to identify Mary as *Theotokos*, the god-bearer. Elizabeth is the first to name the one who will become the mother of the Lord, "the dispossessor."

Mary sings that God has looked with favor upon her low station. God has given honor to her humiliation. I'm struck that the song calls our attention to Mary's social status, pointing us toward her economic and political plight within the degrading occupation of Rome. This is a quality God honors. God calls forth Mary's struggle for survival. These are the words that set before us a prophecy of reversals—high made low, empty made full. God is in the work of overturning the order of the world.

Absent from Mary's Song, Raniero Cantalamessa reminds us, is a metaphysical description of God's nature, of the divine and human intermixing of the baby she bears.[5] No attention is given to atonement or proper trinitiarian formula. The mystery of the incarnation is the power of a child, born into poverty, upending and overturning economies as God's activity in human history. Jesus comes to Mary for women like Mary. God comes for the deliverance of Israel from foreign invaders just as God rose up against Assyria and Babylon. And now God comes in a body into the world of enemies.

These enemies are the proud, the rich, and the mighty—forces that coalesce in Herod as the personification of Israel's enemy, the one who will pursue God's liberator, Jesus, across the pages of the gospel. Mary's song provides a frame of reference for the enemies Jesus will make throughout his life and how these enemies stand in opposition to the flourishing of those at the margins of power. Those who enact the old order through coercive power and excessive wealth are enemies of the reign of God. They are enemies of the reign of God because they are enemies of those who bear that reign in their bodies.[6]

We inherit Mary's song for our own upending. Her song begins in the past, within Israel's history, and continues on, working its way into the social order of Mary's day, as it works its way into our present. Her words are an amalgamation of stories and prophecies, of Israel's redemption and promise. Mary speaks of

God's work that is brought to fruition in Jesus. God will work as God has worked before, now through the extension of fierce love erupting within creation itself, as it was foretold by the prophets. As Jesus' life unfolds, God's purpose is not to install a new regime, to turn the tables so that now the rich are made the servants of the poor. Instead, Jesus will remove the mechanisms of this order entirely.

— — —

THERE IS NO DOUBT that Mary has the empire of Rome in mind as she sings her song. In Judea Herod oversaw what amounted to a police state, heavily taxing the local populace to support his lavish lifestyle and massive building projects. Herod also controlled the appointment of the high priest, which entangled Rome in both temple ritual and political avarice. The high priest was unpopular among ordinary Jews, as the primary qualification for this role was to submit to the will of Herod. In his relatively short rule of Judea, 35 BCE to 4 CE, Herod appointed seven different high priests. One lasted only a day. As Obery Hendricks points out, we can hear the sarcasm in John's remark that Caiaphas was the high priest "that year" (John 11:49).[7]

No distinction between religion and politics existed for people of Jesus' day. People who fell outside the autocratic structure of Roman power and wealth-hoarding were destitute. A small percentage of Rome's population constituted the ultrawealthy. The upper class was comprised of certain tax collectors, temple priests, rich landowners, and the Roman elite. The rest of the populace were peasants, taxed so harshly they scraped by on almost nothing. This created two social classes with those at the bottom inferior in every way.[8] Mary prophesies the end of this arrangement, the upheaval of Rome's despotic and crushing rule.

Because of Mary's bold proclamation, in life and word, against the power of despotism, she is the historic accompanier for women in acts of resistance against the colonization. Christian missionaries upended women's lives by bringing a gospel embedded with gendered hierarchies that restricted social movement. The Ghanaian scholar Mercy Amba Oduyoye writes about the various ways Christian missionaries truncated women's roles in traditional rituals for puberty, marriage, birth, and death, replacing these sacred roles with a male-centric priesthood.[9] Colonization also brought theology that banned culturally normative sexual identities, which shifted social structures and disrupted custom and family formation.

But the Bible in the hands of women spoke to Mary's political and prophetic role as both Jesus' mother and *Theotokos*, mother of God. Mary was an ambivalent figure in the work of colonial dispossession and conquest. The male headship of the Roman Catholic Church twisted the biblical Mary into a model of civility, portraying her as a docile and obedient handmaid. Women were instructed to pattern themselves after Mary's virginity, with an emphasis on her sexual purity. Women thwarted this domestication attempt to colonize Mary's body. "To think about the Virgin Mary as a transgressive symbol," writes Elina Vuola, "means taking the female body as a starting point and a center in itself, not only in the context of how we think of God, Christology, and Mary as an exemplary human being."[10] This revelation returns the politics of Mary to all women.

Mary remains a contested symbol. At times Mary's body was co-opted as an emblem of national conquest. Armies and governments exploited the symbolic power of Mary as the divine-bearing body to give authority to their political repression. She was treated as an object of divine protection for their human project. Statues of Mary were brought onto the battlefield ahead of soldiers in the same way women's bodies are treated as occasionally useful, to be paraded out as honorable but only when they serve patriarchal interests.[11] Ironically, Mary was taken up as a symbol for male dominance and violent overthrow.

But within feminist liberation theologies, Mary is discovered in the bodies of women, not as an ideal, but within their everyday lives. In the ecclesial base community (CEBs) she is not only the mother of God but also "earthly sister, friend of the road (*compañera de camino*), mother of the oppressed, mother of the worthless."[12] Mary brings the ordinary struggle of ordinary women into concert with the divine. She is the bearer of God not in spite of but in the fullness of her experience as a woman. She is full of grace within the community of women—in their child birthing and their menstruation, the disappearing of their children and the hopes of their liberation.

The politics of Mary formed in the life of the COMADRES, the women who organized to locate their sons who were disappeared during El Salvador's protracted civil war. These women organized a collective response to the civil war that plagued their country. Among their actions, they would write letters demanding information from the government as to the whereabouts of their sons. Once they were visited by Archbishop Oscar Romero. Alicia, one of the women, told the story:

> Mons. Romero would read our public letters out loud in his Sunday homily in the Cathedral so that the CoMadres became known nationally. One month before he was assassinated, I remember that Mons. Romero gave us a blessing by

telling us, "Ah, women, you are the Marys of today. Mary spent a long time searching for her son, and you mothers are also walking along the same path that Mary walked. All of you are suffering the same loss, the same pain."[13]

Mary's song calls communities to revolutionary love as they stand against enemies seeking their destruction. All along, while nations rise up, while kings ride to battle, while the rich get richer, while the mighty slaughter their enemies on the battlefield—all along God is at work among the dispossessed to overturn empires.

This confidence that God, the creator of the universe, was on the side of women like the COMADRES was a source of concern to repressive governments. As it was during Mary's time, the governing powers understood the political consequences if common people got ahold of such knowledge. During the British rule of India, the government decided the content of the Magnificat was too politically overt, and it was outlawed from worship. In the 1980s, Mary's Song was banned from public recitation by the Central American juntas. In Argentina, the Mothers of the Plaza de Mayo—those whose children all disappeared during the Dirty War—placed the Magnificat's words on posters throughout the capital plaza. As a result, that military outlawed public displays of Mary's Song.[14]

My favorite image of Mary is the Madonna and Child of Soweto. This icon tells the story of Mary's song breathing power into the anti-apartheid movement of South Africa. The original painting sits in the church of Regina Mundi. Here students gathered to organize against the economic and racial caste system of apartheid. In 1976, during the Soweto uprising, thousands sought shelter in Regina Mundi, hiding between pews

and huddling in the chancel. Apartheid police pursued protestors into the sanctuary, raining down gunfire and teargas.
To this day the church bears the scars of these bullets. Over
the next fifteen years Regina Mundi was the site of organizing.
It became a symbol of hope for Soweto activists. It was also
where many of those killed in the struggle for freedom had their
funerals.[15]

Above the altar is Mary with the skin of a Black South
African. She holds the infant Jesus, who looks like those who
came to Regina Mundi for refuge in hope and in grief. Mary
looks out on the sanctuary and bears witness. She holds the
child, Jesus, but gazes out on the rows of pews, on those killed
by the bullets of their enemies, on those huddling in the chancel, on those weeping over caskets, on those praying and believing (or trying to believe) that another world is possible.

As I read about the funerals held in Regina Mundi, I remem-
bered that Mary's solidarity is constant, even in death. At the
beginning of the story of Jesus, we see mother and child alone.
And at the end, they will be alone again. At the cross, when all
others have fled—when his dying body is abandoned by the
disciples—Mary is one of the women who remain. From the
stable and from the cross, she looks at the Herods and apartheid
regimes, at the colonial conquerors and murderous juntas, and
she warns them that the world does not belong to them. The
power of resistance, of Jesus' body binding human life to the
divine, will upset and reorder the world.

SIX

Love Your Enemies

THE ANGER OF THE PSALMS echoes in Mary's defiance against oppressive regimes. Mary's life, in the collective lives of women and communities of the oppressed, affirms that enemies are potent and formidable. They cause real damage to those who fall into their crosshairs. But in Christianity we do not resolve enmity by destroying our foes or finding middle ground with them. Instead, Jesus ushers in a different system—a new way of living that changes the order of power itself. One of the most formative and quoted texts in the Christian Scriptures is Jesus' teaching as to how the emerging Christian community will act toward enemies:

> But I say to you that listen, Love your enemies, do good to those who hate you, bless those who curse you, pray for those who abuse you. If anyone strikes you on the cheek, offer the other also; and from anyone who takes away your coat do not withhold even your shirt. (Luke 6:27-29)

I've had a front row seat to the damage inflicted by those who utilize the Sermon on the Plain, and its pair in Matthew, as a cudgel to suppress movement work for liberation and the freedom of individuals to escape harmful situations. Jesus' teaching has been deployed to hold women captive to intimate partner abuse and to impede people from reporting sexual assault in the church. It has been weaponized against vulnerable communities who attempt to pull themselves out from under the heel of oppressive power.

Daniel White Hodge, reflecting on the long line of shooting deaths of Black people at the hands of police, writes, "All of this time the use of Christian discourse is used to continue the subjugation of Black bodies in the use of phrases and words such as 'forgive,' 'love your enemies,' and 'bless those that curse you.'"[1] For many, the command to love one's enemy is not a source of freedom but another form of oppression.

James Cone, one of the fathers of Black liberation theology, was often confronted by white people who questioned the methods by which Black liberation would be obtained. Would Cone encourage Black Christians to turn the other cheek? How could he reconcile Black liberation with Jesus' command to "go the extra mile"? "These are favorite *white* questions," writes Cone, "and it is significant that they are almost always addressed to the oppressed and never to the oppressors."[2] Cone goes on to say that white people are only concerned about violence when violence is enacted upon them. Hodge and Cone both point to the hypocrisy of calls to "turn the other cheek" and "forgive" when those who offer these critiques fail to acknowledge or reckon with their own enmeshment in systemic, economic, and social violence. This passive violence most often goes unnamed because it does not involve a fist or a brick.

For Cone, writing with prophetic urgency in the 1970s, to embody the reign of God requires "a total break with the white past" that embodied the destructive forms of the old order. Rather than reversing racial hierarchies or rewiring a few issues, aligning with Jesus' will results in an upheaval of the catastrophic forms of race and class in which we are entangled. We don't need new oppressors, new wealth, or new social classes. We need a new world.

— — —

IN THE GOSPEL OF LUKE Jesus comes down from praying on the mountain. There, at a level place, he turns to see the ordinary people of Judea. The Roman empire is built upon the backs of the peasants sitting on the plain before him, and their bodies litter its streets and ports. Jesus' eyes move over tenant farmers and fishermen, across the faces of widows and beggars. Under the scorching heat of political repression and economic terror, he speaks to them. He tells them to bless and not curse their enemies.

It is one thing to love enemies when they hold no terror over us, when they are no more than a threat to our beliefs or ideologies. It is another thing to bless and not curse those whose intent is to cause destruction. What could Jesus mean by directing these words to the poorest and most vulnerable of the ancient world?

Jesus comes to a people—a blessed people, a beatified people. He turns and asks those who follow him, those who are the embodiment of God's reign, to remove themselves from the hierarchies of power and systems of destruction and instead to make of themselves the embodiment of God's reign. It is only in this new ordering of creation that the distinction between friend and enemy will collapse. This other-worldly vision touches down in the life, death, and resurrection of Jesus. Paulo Freire describes what happens when those crushed by poverty and dispossession discover "that both they and their oppressors are manifestations of dehumanization."[3] It is the work of the gospel to uncover the source of our enmity, to stand fully before it, to confront it, and to be transformed. It is the work of liberation to create the conditions of a world where enemies are freed from enacting harm and victims are freed from receiving it.

It is easier to reduce Jesus' teaching on enemy-love to an ethical injunction, a set of rules we can parcel out to shift our behavior. Instead, Jesus calls us to publicly imagined possibilities of transformation that break open a renewed order. Only then can we love our enemy as we proclaim that their terror no longer has power over us.

— — —

ON THE MORNING of November 11, 1938, German citizens walked the glittering sidewalks of their cities as glass crunched beneath their feet. It was the morning after *Kristallnacht*, the "Night of Broken Glass"—an innocuous name for the decisive moment when the Third Reich shifted from anti-Semitic rhetoric to full-scale repression of the Jewish people in Germany. Over two nights paramilitary forces and civilians set synagogues on fire and destroyed Jewish businesses. The sounds of broken windows and screams echoed across the country.

Dietrich Bonhoeffer, the German theologian, was thousands of miles away. Months earlier, friends and colleagues who were concerned for his well-being had urged Bonhoeffer to leave Germany for the United States. Bonhoeffer spent much of his early career in prewar Germany pondering the theme "love your enemies." This idea operates as the theological center of his early writing: "Christ died for all, murderer and murdered, victim and perpetrator."[4] For Bonhoeffer, Jesus does not come to shut off the church from its enemies. Rather, Jesus dies among enemies. Bonhoeffer writes, "On the Cross he was utterly alone, surrounded by evildoers and mockers. For this cause, he had come, to bring peace to the enemies of God."[5] Following Luther, Bonhoeffer taught that all people are equally in need of forgiveness before a holy God. Because of this our enmities collapse before the throne of God.

By 1942 the language of "love your enemies" dropped almost entirely from Bonhoeffer's writing and teaching. Lori Hale, who studies Bonhoeffer's theology, traces this turn to two events. The first was *Kristallnacht*. Bonhoeffer's anger was ignited both by the act itself and by the silence of moderate clergy who watched from afar. The second event was Bonhoeffer's brief visit to the United States, a decision he regretted, before returning to Germany. Shortly after, Bonhoeffer began work as a courier for the German resistance movement.

One way to understand this shift in Bonhoeffer is to view it as an abandonment of the idealism of Jesus' call to enemy-love in favor of the ethical practicality of standing against the death and destruction of the vulnerable. Immediate concern for the neighbor displaces moralism. We cannot love our enemies and defend those who are vulnerable, and so, when times are difficult, we must choose.

Near the end of his life, in and out of jail for the resistance work that eventually led to his execution, Bonhoeffer began writing a new work—*Ethics*. It was published posthumously and offers a different theological turn. In the Gospels humility, suffering, forgiveness, and love of enemies are not abstractions or ideals. They are concrete—embodied in the person of Jesus Christ. Abstract ideas about love leave us with a pure, untainted form that can never be realized in human life. Instead, writes Bonhoeffer, "The purity of love. . . will not consist in keeping itself apart from the world, but will prove itself precisely in its worldly form."[6] When we read the Sermon on the Mount, the call to enemy-love, we hear not a word to individuals but to people who are responsible for others, for a community or a church resisting the destruction of their neighbors.

In *Ethics*, Bonhoeffer recalls how often Jesus is asked to resolve conflicts, both among his enemies and his disciples. Each time, Jesus resists an either-or interpretation. Instead, he "seems to be answering quite a different question from that which has been put to Him. . . . He speaks with a complete freedom which is not bound by the law of logical alternatives."[7] Jesus is not working within the same structures that everyone else around him assumes is required to navigate the world. More often than not, Jesus' troubling statements to his disciples and followers, be they about money or marriage, treason or taxes, serve as eruptions that shake loose the confines of their imaginations.

— — —

IN MATTHEW'S VERSION of the sermon on the Plain, Jesus' teaching about the form of the beatific community is followed by a series of couplets called the antitheses (Matthew 5:17-20). These teachings compare the religiosity among a sect of Jewish teachers to Jesus' own interpretation of the Torah. Jesus pronounces woe over religious leaders for their public piety, hypocrisy in prayer, and desire for status and wealth. Jesus condemns how religious identity is asserted "through one's accomplishment and religious performance."[8] He explains that our participation in the life of God offers a different way of imagining our identity. Jesus moves us beyond rule-keeping and into the transformation of our collective action.

With Bonhoeffer, I want to move beyond the tension of idealism and practicality in Jesus' instruction on enemy-love. Of all his writings, one of the most significant for me is not Bonhoeffer's formal, published work but a letter he sent to Reinhold Niebuhr about the perilous decision to return to Germany at the height of the Third Reich's power. "I have come to the conclusion that I have made a mistake in coming to America," he writes. "I must live through this difficult period of our national history with the Christian people of Germany."[9] He goes on to explain to Niebuhr, "I will have no right to participate in the reconstruction of Christian life in Germany after the war if I do not share the trials of this time with my people." It is not enough to listen to the call to enemy-love from a distance. Instead, the call of Jesus is to build love in the midst of destruction.

Jesus wills human life into being through love and dies on the cross to reorder creation toward that love. We relocate our participation in the reign of God within the body of Jesus, outside the logical or legal frameworks that we are told determine our good and the good of our enemies. In following Jesus we enact this new imagination, shaping different ways of life.

Jesus does not preach the Sermon on the Plain, the call to enemy-love, in order to deepen our commitment to zealous and harsh demands that conform our wills to humiliation and pain. Interpreting enemy-love as a command to absorb destruction without protest is the source of Karl Marx's critique of the Christianity he saw at work in seventeenth-century Europe. Marx castigated religious practices that placed calls to enemy-love like a veil over the powerless, obscuring their own experience of suffering in a way that distracted them from protesting their terrible working and living conditions. When religion is practiced in a way that makes people comfortable with poor material conditions, when it is "the heart of the heartless condition, the soul of the soulless world," it is no more than an illusion designed to keep people from rising up against those who created these conditions.[10] Marx is right that we need to abolish forms of religion that offer these illusions of "real happiness" as immaterial and spiritual. We are called to a faith where Jesus says to us, "A future has been *given* to you, the air is full of promises, the ship of your life and history itself is sailing toward a harbor where you are expected and your safety is assured. . . . The future has already begun."[11]

— — —

JESUS DOES NOT CALL US to enemy-love for the purpose of making miserable people content with their misery. Neither is enemy-love a way to adjudicate interpersonal conflict. These ways of interpreting the command to love one's enemies blunts the power and force of the gospel. Instead, enemy-love offers to tear apart broken systems and rebuild a world with an imaginative architecture that emerges from lives stayed on liberating love.

In order to build this new way of life, we need these new tools, because as Audre Lorde once wrote, "the master's tools will never dismantle the master's house."[12] These old tools "may allow us temporarily to beat him at his own game, but they will never enable us to bring about genuine change." In her speech to the New York Institute for the Humanities, Lorde speaks about the way white feminists use old tools of patriarchy and racism for social advancement. She calls on white women to address the social and racial stratification between themselves and Black feminists. White feminists need to uncover the forms of power and privilege they inhabit, and to unravel those forms of power in order to make space for a new work of solidarity. Laying down the old tools first requires analysis of how we continue to utilize the apparatus of oppression.

In Jesus' words on enemy-love, I hear Lorde's call to put down the old ways of building and consolidating power. We can no longer concern ourselves with the skirmishes of the empirical guard, allowing this way of ordering society to dominate our lives or take up space in our minds. "This is an old and primary tool of all oppressors," writes Lorde, "to keep the oppressed occupied with the master's concerns."[13] Jesus frees the community on the plain from entrapment to this negotiation of power. The power of the garrison is real and it is also futile. It is destructive and ultimately doomed. For the rest of his life, Jesus will call enemies out of their enmity, into a social order that eradicates the destruction into which they are embedded.

To show us what is possible, Jesus uses examples of how ordinary experiences from common people can subvert social ordering that maintains structures of repression. In the Sermon on the Plain, Jesus is not speaking to equal partners facing tolerable disagreement. Instead, his instructions allude to an oppressive power, a strong group who are controlling the weak. This strong group had the power to force others into service as porters and to steal their clothes without consequence. Jesus had a group in mind: the occupying Roman garrison. Jesus gives this teaching to those who are locked into a system with no exit and no recourse, where survival is determined by submission to the state. To subvert this violence Jesus offers an unexpected protest.

The Roman garrison had unreserved power to coerce and kill. Resistance by refusal ended in massacre as the paranoid and conspiratorial Herod Antipas built an empire of feigned peace called the *Pax Romana*. Into this social order, Jesus called upon the beatified community to refuse the terms of Rome's oppression by putting them on display against the new order. This was an act of rebellion, not against Rome—there will always be another Rome—but against the power of all Romes and all tyrannies that seek to control and repress.

Each time I read that Jesus calls the people gathered on the plain to give up their clothes or carry the pack of a soldier an extra mile, I am reminded that Rome's actions of intimidation and oppression were meant to wear down and overwhelm vulnerable communities. Each time that Rome enacts its methods of coercion, Jesus refuses the terms. In the brutal system of taxation Jesus tells the people to render to Caesar what is Caesar's. Jesus rides into Jerusalem on a donkey to mock the proud and arrogant Caesar who arrives to the city on a war horse. Love of enemies is not sentimentality or emotional manipulation. The reign of God is judgment against the principalities and powers of the dying age.

The description of the beatified community as one that will "turn the other cheek" is directed at a people who already know what it is like to live in the trauma and violence of occupying Rome. Jesus is forming a new people, a body made for a different kind of life together, one designed for freedom and liberation. The followers of Jesus embody this freedom by refusing to reiterate the logic of power that animates the Roman empire.

Rowan Williams reminds us that a member of the Roman garrison slapping a Jewish peasant across the face is not meant to garner a response. This slap is an act of control, of asserting who is in charge. "It's designed to the be the end of the story."[14] To assert oneself in this moment, to turn the other cheek, is to refuse the destructive power that is also destroying one's enemy. It is an act of resistance. Williams writes, "The world of the aggressor, the master, is questioned because the person who is supposed to take no initiative suddenly does."[15] We learn from Gandhi that this response is disconcerting, even frightening for people in power: "It requires courage and imagination: it is essentially that decision *not* to be passive, not to be the victim, but equally not to avoid passivity by simply reproducing what's been done to you."[16] It is, writes Williams, a miracle.

In the teaching to "turn the other cheek" Jesus does not call us to passive reception of violence but instead to dismantle the power of the old order in creative, life-giving ways. This will move us from enemy-love as absorption of violence and toward the form of love James Baldwin describes: "not merely in the personal sense but as a state of being, or a state of grace—not in the infantile American sense of being made happy but in the tough and universal sense of quest and daring and growth."[17] The violence of oppressors will not have the final word because it does not define who we are.

We can see this kind of love in the Gospels as Jesus challenges the prevailing judicial order of his own day. In John's gospel, Jesus offers liberation without violence in the trial of a woman caught in adultery. The legal arbiters of the day bring the woman to Jesus to try out his legal acumen. Already they have harshened the interpretation of Leviticus 20 and Deuteronomy 22, normally understood to require both offending parties to bear the weight of judgment. Yet only the woman appears before the crowd. We see from the outset that gendered power has warped the possibility of justice.

This isn't a story included in the Bible to teach sexual morality. Instead, we see Jesus revoke a legal process dependent upon retribution. The religious leaders demand that Jesus pronounce judgment over the woman. Their demand is a test. Will Jesus oversee her execution or be revealed as an apostate who will not carry out the Law of Moses? As the woman stands, awaiting the outcome, Jesus writes on the ground, ignoring the questions being hurled at him. Eventually, when they refuse to stop questioning him, Jesus responds. "Let anyone among you who is without sin be the first to throw a stone at her" (John 8:7). Slowly, the crowd drops the bricks and rocks they picked up to stone the woman. Then, they walk away.

Jesus, the true judge, next turns to the woman and speaks to her. "Woman, where are they? Has no one condemned you?" When she tells them no one is left, he responds, "Neither do I condemn you. Go your way, and from now on do not sin again" (John 8:10-11).

John Calvin voiced the question of many who read this story. Is it Jesus' intention "to be driving all witnesses away from the witness box and all judges from their bench?"[18] The end of judges and verdicts may be good news for those who suffer under oppressive regimes and unjust laws, but it is frightening for those who demand accountability, who seek arbitration for crimes against them. If Jesus is throwing out all possible judgments, all assessments of right and wrong, tyranny will thrive.

But killing this woman will not correct the wrong committed. Execution reifies the logic that brought this moment of judgment to pass. Instead, Jesus affirms the woman broke the law, then he offers restitution. He instructs the woman to stop her harm. The only way to heal the breach is to release her back to the world, with a directive to hurt others no longer. In this story, enemy-love liberates from death both those who persist in the old order of retribution and punishment and the victim of that order. Jesus returns each person to attend to their participation in social and relational harm.

Karl Barth wrote that Christians engage in the "irrational, impractical, and all together unpractical thing" to love our enemies. "The peculiar interest which in Christian ethics attaches to the love of an enemy is that it is a significant action which announces the Coming World. In doing so, we recognize with our lives that we are bound to the same edict of degradation as our enemies, that the same power of death is working on each of us."[19] Resisting the desire for retribution is the announcement of a new world. It refuses the tools of death. In the end it will save our enemies too.

SEVEN

Undoing Family

THE DISRUPTION OF enemy-love opens us up to new life in an unusual place. Jesus tells his followers that, in living out the reign of God among them, they will become enemies of those most intimate to them. Jesus will cause strife and division within families, upending our political, social, and natural relationships. In the wake of the broken allegiance of kinship, we discover God turning those who were once enemies into family.

Ann Atwater and C.P. Ellis taught me the costliness of following Jesus and how that choice can undo our most intimate relationships and connections. The first story I heard about Ann Atwater begins with a knife. She kept it with her in her handbag, and one day she drew it out in the middle of a city council meeting. The tip of the blade emerged from her clenched, shaking fist as she heard C.P. Ellis spew racist taunts and threats to the city council. With her rage as fuel, Atwater rushed forward, ready to stick the blade into C.P. Ellis's neck.

Fortunately, one of Ann's friends saw the knife in her hand and pulled her back into her seat. "Don't give them the satisfaction," he whispered.[1]

C.P. Ellis was the Grand Cyclops of the local chapter of the Ku Klux Klan. He was infamous for these racist rants and well known for leading white townspeople to revolt against the changes the civil rights movement brought to North Carolina. On the day he spoke to the council, he made sure that everyone could see the handgun tucked into his belt buckle.

The 1970s were a tense time in Durham, North Carolina, the city that both Ann and C.P. called home. A 1964 federal order desegregated schools throughout the United States, but it took a district court order ruling in 1970 to address the segregation of schools in the small southern city of Durham. The local city council decided that the process would begin with a series of meetings where citizens could talk and, hopefully, ease tensions around the desegregation of schools. They chose two people to set the agendas for these meetings, two people who represented the opposite ends of the question around desegregation, two people who could not have been more different. They chose two people who hated each other. They chose C.P. Ellis and Ann Atwater.

Initially, both were hesitant. But the Klan wanted to ensure the decision about desegregating schools included the voice of white supremacy and they convinced C.P. to join. Ann signed on shortly after. They came to the first meeting skeptical and angry, ready for a showdown. Instead, they were surprised. C.P. was shocked to hear the same fear and worries from Black mothers about their children's futures that he heard from white mothers talking about their own children. They were both surprised to discover that people at this meeting had children, both white and Black, who attended poorly performing and underresourced schools. They were amazed to discover that poverty drew their concerns together.

Ten days of meetings and encounters with Ann left C.P. changed. As the official report was given, C.P. stood up before the gathered crowd. He took out his Klan card and tore it into pieces. "If schools are going to be better with me tearing this card up, I will do so," he explained. C.P. went on to be an organizer while Ann worked for the Housing Authority. Their friendship continued for the next thirty years.[2]

People often retell the story of Ann Atwater and C.P. Ellis to remind my local community of the power of reconciliation. In their friendship we witness what happens when we encounter the mutual suffering of another, seeing their fears reflected in our own. Transformation is possible when we set the right terms and open ourselves up to relationship.

I've learned something else from this story. For C.P. Ellis to be made right, he had to uproot himself from the community to which he held a natural allegiance. Ellis left behind family, community, work, and friends. He became their enemy. Despite their common sense of fear for their children's future, Atwater and Ellis were not equally wrong or right. They did not hold firm but different moral ground. The invitation to C.P. was to see himself rightly and to lay down the violence of white supremacy. Only then could he join Ann in her work of desegregating the Durham County public schools.

C.P. Ellis discovered the consequences of choosing this life on the fateful day he tore up his Klan card. This decision would mark him, and the path toward healing was lonely and painful. C.P. felt out of place in Ann's Black church, but he also didn't fit in with middle-class white churches that opposed segregation. Once a fierce and respected leader, he found that following Ann meant dying to who he was before.

Eventually Ellis joined an integrated trade union. But he was shunned from every family reunion. He never found a church that he could call home. When he died, Ann Atwater was the first to arrive at the funeral. Sitting in the front row, the funeral director reminded her that she was sitting in the section reserved for family. "I'm his sister," she replied.

One of my favorite stories about Ann and C.P. is from their first community meeting. They met in the parking lot, and C.P. opened his trunk to show her the .32-caliber revolver he'd covered in blankets. "I come prepared," he told her. Ann pointed at the gun and turned to C.P. She said, "C.P., that's your God." From under her arm she pulled out a worn and heavy Bible. She held it up to his face. "This is mine," she continued. "We'll see which one is stronger."[3]

As it turned out, Ann's was stronger. Ann's gospel is what found its way to C.P., showed him to repent, and showed him he was more than violence and hatred. While I almost always hear that story as uplifting and hopeful, it is also unnerving. The strength of Ann's gospel is that it set C.P. Ellis down in a world in which he could no longer make a life among people who weaponized the violence of hatred and racism. The gospel was strong enough to separate C.P. from everything he knew and loved – his work, his community, his church, his friends, his family. This good news made C.P. a stranger to the old order, and he was strained within it.

Jesus explains that this is what becomes of life for his followers, that the new order of God's love will tear them from their most fundamental relationships:

Do you think that I have come to bring peace to the
earth? No, I tell you, but rather division! From now on,
five in one household will be divided, three against two
and two against three; they will be divided:
> father against son
>> and son against father,
> mother against daughter
>> and daughter against mother,
> mother-in-law against her daughter-in-law
>> and daughter-in-law against mother-in-law.
(Luke 12:51-53)

E.P. Sanders once wrote that the most offensive innovation of
Jesus' interpretation of the Mosaic law is the command for a man
to immediately join the mission rather than staying to bury his
father (Luke 9:59-60).[4] In the first century, someone who refused
to take up this obligation was so far outside the bounds of culture
that they would be considered ethically and morally disgusting.
But there are times when Jewish tradition relativizes family commitment if that commitment conflicts with obedience to God
and keeping the law. We see this in the book of Maccabees where
brothers agonize over a decision to face martyrdom despite their
longing to remain with family (4 Maccabees 13:19, 27; 14:1).

Jesus intensifies this already existing impulse within Judaism.
He prophesies a reign of God that will break apart families as
with a sword. This is another instance when Jesus offers shocking interpretations of the Hebrew Scriptures that often leave his
own disciples flabbergasted. Not only is Jesus often uninterested in ending conflict but here he also tells his disciples they will
make enemies in following him. Jesus reveals that opposition to
the gift of a renewed social order, the reign of God, will cut into
the very marrow of human life by separating kin.

We are at a disadvantage in understanding Jesus' intention in his powerful and consistent renunciation of family if we assume the family is shaped only by love or care, or that it exists to uphold virtue or maintain morality. Family was and continues to be a form of politics that sustains a form of economic and social life. In the ancient world, the primary role of the family was to produce what was needed to survive and to continue that line into the future. "Marriage, therefore, is a legal and social contract between two families for the promotion of the status of each, and the appropriate preservation and transferal of property to the next generation," write Carolyn Osiek and David Balch.[5] Families are the basic unit of a social system first, even as they produce strong emotional and spiritual bonds.

Family in the first-century Greco-Roman world was such a powerful institution within that larger system that it could override Roman dictates and identity. *Familia* in the Roman context was more complex than nuclear or even extended families in the west and included patron-client relationships, slaves, children as contributors to the household economy, and the unification of property through marriage. Households "underpinned kingdom, serving as a micro version of the state," writes Jeremy Punt.[6] Family was part of the broader hierarchy of Roman empire with the emperor at the top.

It's difficult to make comparisons between ancient families and our contemporary experience of family. But we can attend to how family, in any age, is structured by economic and political life. We may like to think that our families are immune from being a part of the struggles of work or politics that happen outside our homes. But Jesus makes it clear that the reign of God will find its way into the intimate places of human existence because there is no "outside" to coercive power.

Jesus doesn't believe in arbitrarily hurting human relationships. Instead, we are pulled out of old ways of life, and that, in turn, changes every part of our existence.

Our families are not neutral enclaves, freed from economic consideration—as any working mother will tell you. Our family structures have genealogies. Their shapes change over time in response to the economics of our culture. This is true for those of us alive today, just as it was in the first century. In the United States, capitalism produces and requires monogamous, heterosexual families that create offspring. Linn Tonstad reminds us that, in this social vision, "children must be born, clothed, fed, and educated, so that they, in turn, become productive workers and consumers."[7] Parents of these children—not society as a whole, which benefits from their labor—take on the financial responsibility to raise these children.

The same is true for private property. We justify acquiring and keeping private property because we intend to hand it down to our children. Tonstad writes, "The point of the nuclear family in contemporary capitalism is to ensure that private property will share the apparent non-economic status of the family, its social location as a form beyond capital."[8] In addition, there needs to be a good reason for working-class people to perform their monotonous, underpaid, often dangerous work, one that outweighs the logic of terrible working conditions and a stagnant minimum wage—work that is insufficient to produce a good life.

The care and support of the family we financially support is the reward, we are told. We are instructed to claim the nuclear family as love, care, support, and nurture, untouched by the realities of the workplace. In turn, workers need someone to cook, clean, and nurture children, as they participate in producing capital for the business owners and bankers. A wife often fills this role, or an underpaid worker who is willing to work as a caretaker for other people's children in order to provide for her own. This system requires economic classes built on racial categories—those who benefit from this system and those who are taken advantage of by this system. Family is no less a part of the economic fabric of our time than it was in the ancient world.

Jesus inserts a disruption. He calls us out of systems of primary loyalty to our kin and binds us to those to whom we have no natural relation and from whom we can extract no economic benefit. This theme runs the length of Luke's gospel. The family as kinship system is upended and replaced with those who have also disrupted their lives to follow Jesus. In the wake of natural or social family systems, Jesus creates a new society, a group of people who find their way to one another and reformulate as the family of God. There is no equivocation on Jesus' part. With growing intensity, he asserts this teaching throughout the gospel. "Whoever comes to me and does not hate father and mother, wife and children, brothers and sisters, yes, and even life itself, cannot be my disciple" (Luke 14:26), Jesus pronounces with profound seriousness.

In the meal narratives we see Jesus upset the social allegiance of family. More than potlucks or nightly dinners, meals in the ancient world were a form of social ordering that included an extended network of patron-client relationships. Patronage created extended family in "a mutual relationship between unequals for the exchange of services and goods."[9] In a society where people could not trust the government for their well-being, patronage created a system of informal friendship and kinship ties to spread a social safety net. It was part of the structure of the ancient family.

This structure exacerbated social hierarchies; "it necessarily fosters unequal relationships and undermines horizontal ones."[10] In the United States we prize a distinction between private and public, social and political. The truth is that these spheres of life we think of as distinct are tied to and reinforce one another. In the ancient Roman world a wealthy and powerful patron would extend his benefaction to a lower-class client, and that client offered their loyalty and obedience in return. This included public praise in the form of statues and inscriptions. Patrons sat in places of honor at public ceremonies and councils. In exchange, the patron granted favors and gifts to clients. As we've seen, in first-century Judea, the enormous class difference left most people struggling to survive day-to-day and a few wealthy aristocrats benefitting from their taxation and production.

Meals offered clients the opportunity for social advancement. An invitation to dinner was the primary vehicle for changing one's social status, placing a would-be client in the orbit of a patron. But this required keen attention to and management of one's place. In Luke 14, Jesus tells the story of a meal-as-social-advancement. Jesus explains how this sort of event usually works. At a banquet, people of lower status step aside in order to let those of higher status have the places of honor. Jesus subverts this practice as he introduces a form of life where the goal is to take the place of lower honor. God, the true patron, welcomes us into a place of the only honor that matters, participation in the reign of God.

The parable continues as Jesus tells those seated, those who have the edge on economic advancement:

> When you give a luncheon or a dinner, do not invite your friends or your brothers or your relatives or rich neighbors,

in case they may invite you in return, and you would be repaid. But when you give a banquet, invite the poor, the crippled, the lame, and the blind. And you will be blessed, because they cannot repay you, for you will be repaid at the resurrection of the righteous. (Luke 14:12-14)

It is preposterous to suggest family is a place that is not defined by social hierarchy. It is unthinkable that people who can provide no social capital would be given entrance before those who can bolster the profile of the host. It is, at its core, the abolition of family as they know it.

After both the first and second elections in which Donald Trump ran, I heard white people express concern about family members who voted for the Republican presidential candidate. For some it became a break in the dam. They realized their family members had silently harbored racist and xenophobic beliefs. The people who raised them justified child separation at the border. Their family members expressed concerns for Christian religious freedom and a desire to secure a Supreme Court that would overturn the right to a safe and legal abortion. These issues overrode compassion for human suffering. But at the end of the day, I heard the same reply. "They are still family." You had to tolerate racism and bigotry at the Thanksgiving table, even if you believed your family was wrong.

As you have intuited, this is not a prescriptive book, offering rules about words you ought to say to your bigoted sister or your father who is enmeshed in anti-Semitic conspiracy theories. But I do hope that, as Christians, we live as people grounded in the life of Jesus. From him we learn that aligning our lives with God's order will lead to equally powerful reactions, including rejection by one's family. "Do not think that I have come to bring peace to the earth," Jesus tells a shocked crowd. "I have not come to bring peace but a sword" (Matthew 10:34). The peacemaking Jesus intends for the disciples invites conflict in every area of our lives. Throughout the Gospels, Jesus models this in a life of making enemies.

The sword of Jesus' good news is one that pierces natural allegiances. Instead of focusing on the family, Jesus draws together those who were separated by ethnic and social hierarchies —Jews and Gentiles, slave and free, and people across the spectrum of gender and sexual identity. These identities are not erased. Instead, some of us are invited to join others where they are, to reshape our bodies away from the corruptions of Mammon and state violence, and to take our place among those at the margins of dominant and violent power. Jesus invites people who live lives of "woes" to join those who are "blessed."

– – –

IN THE NEW TESTAMENT, conflicts with family are related to conflicts over money. After Jesus tells the disciples that anyone who does not hate mother and father, and even life itself, cannot follow him, Jesus offers another outrageous teaching—the disciples will also need to give up their possessions. He expects the disciples to leave behind a life that binds them to social hierarchy, hoarding wealth, and taking advantage of others. That life is incompatible with the reign of God.

For Jesus, enmity within family groups is an inevitable consequence within the profound rupture with the old order. But there is tension too. The Hebrew Bible commands us to honor our parents, without exception for their bad behavior. Jesus doesn't abandon this command. He widens and shifts its scope.

In Matthew, Jesus becomes angry with the Pharisees because he knows they turn over their wealth to the temple rather than using it to support their parents (Matthew 15). The Pharisees' interpretation of the law allows them to rededicate their property to the temple treasury, assuring it will be off limits for use by others, including elderly parents.[11] Jesus is in line with the broader opinion of Judaism of the day, where the obligation to care for parents is taken with utmost seriousness.[12] His anger is aimed at this particular innovative sect who use the Mosaic law to protect wealth rather than attending to the heart of the law—that we are called to provide for vulnerable people, including aging parents.

The reign of God will challenge old ideas about who our enemies are, about the people to whom we owe allegiance, even those we call family. And it will deepen our commitment to care for the vulnerable, whether they are bound to us by kinship or by choosing to be members of the same body, the church. The force of the gospel is so profound that it will dismantle old enmities and create new ones in its wake. The reorientation of ourselves around family is a place of shifting and realigning, rather than a static institution. Family is expansive. It is *familia*.

Theologian Justo González explains that the change from *familia* to family is one of the more painful and perplexing processes of migration. "Here," writes González of the United States, "a family is a nuclear group, usually composed of those who live or grew up under the same roof—most commonly, parents and children. There, the *familia* was a complex network of relatives by blood, by marriage, and even by baptism."[13] Dominant white culture in the United States works to maintain the centrality of the nuclear family over an unruly, often shifting and expanding organism of *familia*.

González explains that it isn't difficult to make the transition to the church as the location of *familia*, "a conglomeration of families—traditional families of parents and children, as well as non-traditional families of single people, same-sex couples, etc."[14] If *familia* is an "ever widening circle of people" who are committed to shared life and to one another's flourishing, belonging escapes the boundaries assumed by birth or marriage allegiances. In this strange world of Jesus, the strongest tie is not to blood but those who also follow the reimagined social and political world of God's flourishing.

It is this impulse that led the *mujerista* theologian Ada María Isasi-Díaz to utilize the term "kin-dom of God" as a foil to the "kingdom of God" with its embedded metaphor of nationalism, hierarchy, and patriarchal dominance. For Latinas, she wrote, kin-dom offers a description of liberation that is "self-determining" within an interconnected community, seeing God's movement emerge from *la familia*, from the family God makes among strangers who are brought into new forms of economic and political kinship.

Kin-dom became the term she used to describe God's *libertad*, the liberation of God at work among people, the good news for those who suffer at the hands of kings and their kingdoms. Isasi-Díaz dedicated her life to the work of *mujerista* theology, where the center of theological study is born from the experience of Latinas. She writes that, for Latinas, this liberation emerges from opening up space where love invites us into kinship. As we join others, the table of our belonging grows. Liberation is found not in hope deferred to another world, to life after death, but in what can be created now.

Mujeristas utilize the language of kin-dom to describe the way in which God's liberation happens within us, in the most intimate spaces of human economy. At the Last Supper, Jesus gathers the disciples for Passover. Instead of dispersing his followers to their biological families or to the households constructed for economic leverage, Jesus gathers a new people. Once strangers, they join together, passing the cups of Passover wine and breaking the bread—*la familia de Dios*.

Mujerista kin-dom language weaves together the prediction that we will become enemies to our kin with the promise of a new family made up of those united in the mission of Jesus. We move from concerns about imperialistic "loss of family values" to a vision of family within a broad and ever-shifting belonging "that has to do not exclusively with blood-relatives but also with those who are united by bonds of friendship, of love and care, of community."[15] In this expansive, hopeful way of social reordering, we experience "a sense of belonging and being safe, to be and become fully oneself."[16]

For people rejected by family because of their sexual identity, for those whose home life is marked by negotiation between tolerance and duty—often family of origin has ceased to be a place of belonging long ago. Instead of reforming the family or piecing together a life at odds with our deepest identity, Jesus turns us toward others. Isasi-Díaz hears a new response to the question posed by Jesus, "Who do you say I am?" "Latinas answer Jesus," Isasi- Díaz writes:

> You are my brother, my sister, my mother and my father, my grandmother, aunt, uncle, *comadre* and *copadre*, who stands with me and who struggles with me. You are amazingly special to me because I am amazingly special to you. You are my big brother protecting me, and you are my little sister whom I protect. You are my husband, my wife, my

partner, my significant other for whom I am precious and who loves me unconditionally. You and I are family, Jesus. What more can you be for me? What more do you want me to be for you?[17]

The shift from nuclear family to *familia de Dios* is significant because family is a *polis,* a social unit within a larger political vessel.

For many people, family is a significant source of pleasure, joy, and comfort. It may be unnerving to consider a potential tear could result from following the way of Jesus. I have no doubt that the power of familial bonds to override all other loyalties is what Jesus calls into question, much to the shock of his disciples. Jesus' life is a kind of apocalypse, an unveiling of that which we take for granted. He unsettles the unexamined—this is the revelation. We are each called out of the safety and assumption of unity with our kin, often thin and veiled, and into a new life among strangers who will become for us and for creation *la familia de Dios.*

Know Your Enemy

IN THE GOSPELS we watch conflict erupt within a different family, the family of Judaism. Unlike the enmity between the Jewish people and the Herods of this world, I find this enmity a source of discomfort and pain. One reason for this is that the Jewish people in my life are a source of hope for our broken world. They are the organizers of Carolina Jews for Justice who show up each time we are called upon as religious communities to organize for social change. Over the years I have been awed by the work of Rabbis for Human Rights, who utilize legal channels to stop the seizure of Palestinian land and to advocate for Palestinian agricultural rights.

Whenever there is mention of Jews in the New Testament my mind turns not to enemies, but to my friends Eric and Jenny Solomon, co-rabbis at our local synagogue. One Saturday they invited me to offer the Shabbat message. I arrived early at Beth Meyer synagogue and waited outside the bulletproof glass windows. A few minutes later, I was greeted by two men who swept the building before it opened for worship. It was then I noticed that the security guards each held long sticks with mirrors attached to the ends. I asked a greeter what the mirrors were for. "During the holidays the guards look under each of the cars in the parking lot," she said. They were checking for explosives.

A long and horrific pattern of anti-Semitism has led to the need for those mirrors, and this anti-Semitism is rooted in the history of the church. It took shape in pogroms, legal crack-downs, and forced conversions. The church fueled violence against Jewish people through stereotypes of greed and theft, buttressed by the growing power of the Catholic and Protestant churches in Europe. The historic church has been devastating for Jews, advancing a theology of misappropriated enmity that has resulted in persecution and violence over our two-thousand-year history.[1]

The church created and exacerbated the lie of Jewish otherness with deadly consequences. The church's role in the decimation of Jewish people spans the decades—from the Crusades to the Inquisition, from Russian pogroms to the Shoah. Those poison roots stretch into the present. In October 2018, a man broke into the Tree of Life Synagogue in Pittsburgh, Pennsylvania, and shouted, "All Jews must die!" before he opened fire. He killed eleven people and injured six more. The man, it was later discovered, was part of the Christian nationalist movement that claims a worldwide Jewish conspiracy is at work to bring an end to Christianity. The church has taken differences and turned them into weapons used to dominate and destroy.

After I offered the Shabbat message, the leaves bright and full in the windows behind me, Rabbi Eric ended the service with the kaddish, the prayer of mourning for the dead. But this week, Rabbi Eric told us, rather than having those who recently lost a loved one recite the kaddish, we would say it together. In unison we stood and read in Aramaic: "May God's majesty be revealed in the days of our lifetime and the life of all Israel—speedily, imminently, To which we say: Amen."[2]

Despite being a prayer of mourning, the words of the kaddish don't mention death. The words of the prayer affirm God's persistent love, God's mercy that extends throughout all time, even when hope seems lost. On that Shabbat we said the kaddish for those murdered at the Tree of Life massacre. But there were more people to include, more deaths rendered from unattended hate. Together we prayed the kaddish for the Jewish people killed in an anti-Semitic attack only the day before, at a kosher food market in Jersey City, New Jersey. We held silence for a moment, as the consequences of enmity washed over us.

— — —

TODAY JUDAISM AND CHRISTIANITY are separate religions. Jews and Christians are co-readers of the same Hebrew Scriptures but with different interpretations of those Scriptures as well as distinct practices and communities. In the New Testament this division did not yet exist. When we hear John's gospel worry for the disciples and their "fear of the Jews," when we encounter Jesus' indictment of temple practices and his engagement in debate with religious leaders—if we import differences that developed over centuries into our reading of the Bible, we open ourselves up to making enemies built on misinformation.

When enmity slips in through falsification of difference, this deception turns deadly. By some estimates, it took four hundred years for Christianity and Judaism to work out discrete identities. We can imagine these as communities in flux, "the ways that often parted."[3] Even then, some religious leaders had to work diligently to keep up robust and separate Jewish and Christian identities, with common people attempting to reduce the difference in their daily lives.

To understand enmity in Jesus' ministry, its contours and limits, its complications and possibilities, we have to position ourselves rightly with respect to the conflicts that emerge throughout Jesus' life. In the first centuries, when the Gospels are being written (most within decades of Jesus' life, death, and resurrection), we witness conversations internal to a community. We meet people working out identity as different groups rooted in common traditions, grappling with the same historic catastrophes—the destruction of the temple, persecution as religious minorities, and the fall of Rome.

At times, the New Testament retains an overly simplistic and ultimately false claim that the Jews killed Jesus (1 Thessalonians 2:14-15). The crucifixion narrative in Matthew includes one such indictment, claiming "the Jews" have Jesus' blood on their hands. Instances like these are reminders of the blunt force of anti-Judaism in the burgeoning church, borne out of conflict, fear, and anger. I won't erase the times when the New Testament participates in a violence at odds with the good news it claims to profess. The hope of a peaceable future depends upon confronting our own anti-Jewish texts and on how anti-Jewish readings of the New Testament have been handed down to us.

— — —

RATHER THAN DISMISSING Judaism, the New Testament introduces us to Jewish Jesus, who is circumcised on the eighth day, trained in Torah, an observer of ritual purity laws, a wearer of tallit, and a keeper of the Sabbath. Despite this presentation of Jesus' stalwart commitment to the Mosaic law, a persistent strain in the church is convinced Jesus' purpose is to end the legalism of Judaism with its seemingly overbearing and harsh requirements. In this interpretation, Jesus is Jewish but only to a certain extent.

But reading the New Testament this way assumes a Christian distinction from Judaism that did not exist in the first century. Instead, just as Christianity exists today in multiple traditions, Judaism existed in a variety of forms. These groups often disagreed about how to most faithfully live out the Mosaic law. Just as in the church, those disagreements grew intense and heated.

Because the New Testament often ties together narratives about the Pharisees, Sadducees, and scribes, it's easy for readers today to conflate these groups. In reality, in the ancient world we see distinctive sects within Judaism, and they were often in contentious relationship with one another. The Dead Sea Scrolls describe the life of one Jewish sect called the Qumran community. In the scrolls, the Qumran community come up with biting monikers and insults to describe other Jewish groups.

They call one of the groups "the seekers of smooth things." According to Qumran, the Seekers are wrong in their interpretation of the law, dangerously so. These Seekers, they claim, looked for any easy way out of the law. We can sum up the disagreement this way: "Our foes act as if they are searching the Torah for the appropriate rules of conduct, but what they are doing is looking for deceptive teachings, slippery ways around what the Torah requires, not the real meaning and full implications entailed by the law of Moses."[4] Most scholars believe the people of Qumran are describing a sect called the Pharisees. Like other Jews of his day, Jesus also levels criticism against the way certain members of this particular sect innovated the law.

But even here we should exercise caution. Joel Marcus reminds us that, in the ancient context, a hypocrite is "a person whose interpretation of the Law differs from one's own."[5] In the New Testament, we observe this intercommunity debate regarding different ways multiple groups are teaching others how to keep the law of Moses.

Jesus does not use the tenor of conversation we would for interreligious dialogue—the careful, gentle work of relationship-building across difference, the work of respect and the desire to know one another as people bound to mutual hopes of peace and justice. Jesus' enmity toward the Jewish religious leaders takes on a different tone because it is conversation within the family of Israel. The leaders who end up most often on the receiving end of Jesus' wrath are the Pharisees. The problem from Jesus' perspective is that these Jewish leaders block ordinary people from practicing the life-giving law. These kinds of accusations are not unique to Jesus, nor is the rancorous mood of his debates.

The Pharisees were a reform movement within Judaism, innovators who actively sought out others to participate in their new way of keeping the law. Jesus is not frustrated with the Pharisees because they want to keep the law. "Jesus' Judaism," writes the Jewish scholar Daniel Boyarin, "was a conservative reaction against some radical innovations in the Law stemming from the Pharisees and the Scribes of Jerusalem."[6] Jesus reacts to a specific reform movement and its interpretive changes.

We can better understand Jesus' critique of the reform movement of Pharisaism in a homily in which Jesus explains to a crowd that "there is nothing outside a person that by going in can defile, but the things that come out are what defile" (Mark 7:15). We also learn that, in saying this, "He declared all foods clean." What comes out defiles—adultery, pride, slander, and envy. Daniel Boyarin relays Jesus' intention: "Why does the Torah only render impure that which comes out and not that which goes in, if not to teach us something, namely, that morality is more important than the purity rules—and especially Pharisaic extension of them?"[7] When it comes to the law, Jesus wants "to deepen our commitment both to practicing it and to incorporating its meanings."[8] Jesus does not intend to distinguish, as Luther did, between the "spirit and the letter of the law." Instead, Jesus' intention is to help fellow Jews live out the life-giving torah by interpreting the law from within his own authoritative teaching.

I offer a warning against false caricatures of Judaism that pit Jesus against the system of ritual purity and temple sacrifice. Christians may find it hopeful to portray Jesus as the one who overcomes the legalism of purity, who crosses boundaries that Jewish people held in place to stop intermixing. But in advancing this kind of "freedom," Judaism itself becomes the enemy.

In a careful reading of the Gospels, we see that Jesus does not terminate ritual purity laws or dismiss Jewish legal practice. Jesus' criticisms are clear and resounding for certain religious leaders, but not because of these teachers' desire to uphold the Mosaic law. We're in a better position to understand Jesus' relationship to the religious teachers if we distinguish between ritual purity and sinfulness. According to the logic of Mosaic law, people could be both ritually impure and holy. Because of the extent of normal, everyday activities and bodily functions that made someone impure, most Jewish people were likely impure most of the time. Ritual bathing provided the solution to impurity but not to sin.

Impurity became a moral problem when it entered into the holy space of the temple. Once a certain amount of contagion entered the temple, God could no longer be present there. When people purposefully brought impurity into the sacred places, impurity turned to sin. The ritual purity system was not a way to keep people in their place. It was designed for compassion, "a protective and benevolent system intended to preserve God's presence among his people."[9] Rather than being a burden or a source of harm or shame, the law was, and is, life and grace. It offers a way to identify and combat the old order of sin and death that, through human sinfulness, manifests itself in a good and holy creation.

Matthew Thiessen explains that Jesus comes to eliminate the source of contagion itself, the forces of death at the root of impurity. Each time Jesus appears to be breaking a boundary, moving into the space of the impure, he works to bring an end to the cause of impurity. In the gospel of Mark, Jesus' ministry is an assault on the powers of the old age, from illness to demonic forces to death. "God has introduced something *new* into the world to deal with the sources of these impurities: Jesus," Thiessen reminds us.[10] The power of Jesus' ability to stop death leaks from his body. And in the end, Jesus will overcome death itself.

— — —

IN MATTHEW WE first meet the Pharisees when they come to John for ritual immersion. He greets them with judgment, comparing them to a bucket of snakes. They are a mess of anger and poison, lashing out and stinging. John seethes, "You brood of vipers! Who warned you to flee from the wrath to come?"

(Matthew 3:7). John doesn't come up with this stinging insult on his own. The prophets before him were as clear and vicious in describing the trouble that the powerful make for the powerless in Israel:

> They hatch adders' eggs,
>   and weave the spider's web;
> whoever eats their eggs dies,
>   and the crushed egg hatches out a viper. (Isaiah 59:5)

The Sadducees and Pharisees have come together to scout out the ritual bathing occurring at the Jordan River. From the very beginning of the gospel, we see the problem of the Pharisees' innovations. John responds in anger. He tells the religious leaders that their expectation of ritual bathing to fulfill a requirement is not enough. This immersion for purity should lead to a new life, one that produces good fruit. As we'll see in the rest of Matthew, according to Jesus, the Pharisees do the opposite.

The most prominent and intense moment of enmity with the Pharisees, along with the scribes, continues on the theme of hypocrisy. In Matthew 23, Jesus pronounces a series of "woes." Jesus hurls these insults as a verdict of judgment on the particular way that the Pharisees and scribes interpret the law. The rabbis who proceed from the Pharisees continued to debate the questions of how to fulfill the requirements of the law through the two houses of Shammai and Hillel, rabbis who lived and taught at the same time as Jesus. The Talmud reminds us that, during the time of Hillel and Shammai, "dispute proliferated among the Jewish people and the Torah became like two Torahs."[11] Even Pharisaic Judaism was more complicated than the New Testament lets on.

Regardless, Jesus' contention in the series of "woes" concerns the actions of the Pharisees and scribes *in conflict* with their own teachings. Remarkably, at one point, Jesus tells his listeners that they should do what the Pharisees teach but should avoid acting like them. Matthew's Jesus is angry at the expectations these teachers place on ordinary people, which are burdens that the Pharisees will not endure themselves. He's angry at their public displays of piety as well as their desire for recognition and positions of honor.

The "woes" expand upon this judgment. Ironically, through their innovations of the law, the scribes and Pharisees prevent people from being able to keep the law. Jesus sees them embroiled in what appear to him unnecessary and trivial legal debates. Next, the Pharisees exasperate Jesus with the extra effort of tithing on herbs but ignoring "weightier matters" (Matthew 23:23). Over and over, the judgment falls in the same place—observing the law without attending to the heart of the matter.

— — —

IN THE NEW TESTAMENT we are onlookers at an internal conversation between two parties who are interconnected by their religious and ethnic tradition. It is not novel for a prophet, an insider to the people of Israel, to be critical of their own leaders—the priests, kings, and judges who were trusted to lead and rule over Israel. The final "woe" from Jesus names the role of the prophet, those in Israel's history who act like Jesus by calling their own people to repentance through judgment. Throughout the history of Israel, from Abel to Zechariah, sin and destruction in the community is called out by those who attempt to bring Israel back into right covenantal relationship with God.

The purpose of pointedly naming the behavior of Israel's religious leaders is not for destruction. Prophecies name God's judgment, not human judgment. The announcement of charges against leaders who make life unbearable for ordinary Israelites is a consistent theme of the Hebrew scriptures. Isaiah launches with an invective aimed at the action of priests and kings who offer lavish burnt offerings even as the community is under siege. The vulnerable fight off starvation while the priests eat well:

> Trample my courts no more;
> bringing offerings is futile;
>   incense is an abomination to me.
> New moon and sabbath and calling of convocation—
>   I cannot endure solemn assemblies with iniquity.
> (Isaiah 1:12b-13)

This is not the prophet announcing the end of the sacrificial system of the temple. These words are pointed at the elite, the decision-makers, and those charged with protecting and providing for the economically and socially vulnerable. Whatever is behind the decision to ramp up the number of sacrifices, God is incensed that leaders would diligently keep religious festivals that threaten people who could be eating the food that turns to ash on the altar. While lavish sacrifices are unfolding in the temple, widows and working people go hungry. The people behind this injustice have blood on their hands (Isaiah 1:15). The God who desires "mercy and not sacrifice" is the same in the Old Testament and the New. Jesus comes in the line of prophets before him.

As it is, in the New Testament and in the Hebrew Scriptures, God is not eternally patient. The Old Testament does not allow for the endless possibility of removing one's self from the destruction of others. God issues both mercy and judgment. At a certain point, thankfully, judgment passes and God does "a new thing" (Isaiah 43:18-19). In Isaiah, these judgments are purposeful. God steps in to end the destructive rule that threatens the people of Israel who are vulnerable to the poor decision-making, gluttony, and territorial expansion of their leaders (Isaiah 5).

— — —

IF WE ARE TO HAVE enemies well, we first need to understand them. When the church assumes that one of many sectarian groups in the ancient world is a stand-in for all Jews, we distort enmity. When we turn Jesus' rancor for one sect's version of law-keeping into abrogation of the law of Moses, we lose out on the hopeful possibility of what we can discover for ourselves in these conflicts. Disinformation is a scandalous source of enmity. When prejudice and assumptions define the cause of our strife, we have departed from the gospel. The church falsely made an enemy of Judaism. In doing so, we perpetuated lies that justified genocide, forced removal, and violence against individuals and communities. We distracted ourselves from the heart of Jesus' teachings and how those teachings reflect back on each of us.

In the New Testament we discover quite a bit about the way enmity takes shape within communities of shared religious and ethnic identity. It isn't unusual for our most intense conflicts to occur with those closest to us, those with whom we share much in common. The church in the United States is a witness to these profound and often hostile divisions and church splits. Our differences can be stark, our conflicts formidable. Divisions within the church over women's ordination, LGBTQ inclusion, and responses to racism are no small matter. But understanding our differences, getting to the heart of our conflicts, is complex work that requires vigilance within ourselves, knowledge of our histories, and honesty about the shape of power within our communities.

When we fail to do this work, our response to relationships of conflict falls somewhere between two well-worn paths. The first is to assume that anyone different from me is an enemy, that every person who does not share my commitments, values, or beliefs is a threat to that for which I've worked and that which I love. Anyone who stands in the way of my commitments must be eliminated. This way of approaching conflict instills suspicion, fear, and prejudice. It leads to the violence and destruction that we see in the anti-Semitism fomented by the church for centuries.

But there is another approach to "others as enemies." In this way of calculating conflict, people who harm others are either misunderstood or simply acting out of their own self-interest to protect their thriving. The way to overcome our enmity is by creating spaces where the falsehood of being enemies is unmasked. We will discover that we all want the same things—we simply have different ways of reaching those goals. Once we are able to unite around this set of shared expectations, we can put down our more radical ideas and work toward a mutually agreed upon goal.

The Jewish Jesus among the Jewish Pharisees challenges both ways of having enemies. Our disagreements can be real. They can be heated and intense, but the task is to accurately name these conflicts rather than falling back into tropes that distort the position that is not our own. Sometimes, as with the Jewish people, we learn that our differences can become the grounds for violence and destruction. In reality, Jews and Christians can hold space for our differences and our common hopes for peace and justice without compromising either.

At other times, when we are in conflict with people in our tradition, we can commit to both humanizing our enemies and working against the ways our differences lead to the subjugation and suffering of others. The work for each of us is to discern the limits of difference and recognize when power turns these differences to enmity. In all of this, we are called to live into the truth that all people, even our enemies, are made in the image of God. Our longing is for a world that frees each of us from the destruction of hate and harm.

The Talmud tells a story that reminds us how much Christians can learn from our Jewish siblings and their commitment to peace. In the story, Rabbi Meir is so distressed about the havoc caused by delinquents in his neighborhood that he can imagine no other mercy than for God to cause them to die. His wife, Beruriah, overhears this and wonders how he has come to believe such a prayer is permitted. Perhaps Rabbi Meir is thinking of Psalm 104. So Beruriah reinterprets the psalm for her husband. Rather than causing the wicked "to be no more" (Psalm 104:35) through death, God intends something else. Beruriah explains that the hope for the criminals in their neighborhood comes in a different prayer: "'Pray for them that they should repent, and there will be no more wicked people.'"

He prayed for them, and they repented. [12]

NINE

Jesus Draws the Line

JESUS' ANGER AT the practices of his fellow Jews, the Pharisees, is one way we can learn to differentiate between difference and enmity, and how we can grapple with the cost when we do not discern well. But how do we know if we are correct? Everyone who acts in the name of God believes they are on God's side. We may think we're acting as we ought to, but the question lingers: how do we know?

We will wait a long time if we seek unencumbered moral clarity in naming our enemies and working against the harm they cause to us and others. With fifty years of hindsight, most of us can say without equivocation that God was against a system of education that segregated white and Black children, miring generations of Black children in poverty through lack of opportunity and resources. But white people today often overstate the clearness of the moral charge of the modern civil rights movement. During the 1960s, the majority of white people in the United States opposed the freedom rides and sit-ins. Critics questioned the ethics of the movement's tactics. These critics charged that movement leaders garnered change by inflaming tensions and inciting violence. Martin Luther King Jr. once earned a 60 percent disapproval rating in a national poll.[1]

The political victory over Jim Crow oppression was not an obvious moral good to the nation as a whole at the time. Predominately white churches often stood to the side or actively opposed the movement. Anti-racism was not evident in a plain text reading of the Bible for the majority of these white Christians. It was within this context that Martin Luther King Jr. wrote his "Letter from a Birmingham Jail," castigating moderate white Christian and Jewish clergy who implored King to wait, to negotiate, and to stop actions that incited violent reactions. Instead of finding support and encouragement from clergy, King wrote, "The white ministers, priests, and rabbis of the South. . . have been outright opponents, refusing to understand the freedom movement and misrepresenting its leaders."[2] The questions before us—how we are to stand with Jesus and how we are to listen for our call to action—are no more clear today than they were in the 1960s.

— — —

I AM SENSITIVE to the lack of clarity around our choices, our enemies, and the consequences of choices made, because my story is enmeshed in this difficult task. I grew up in a conservative Episcopal church, now a part of the Anglican Church in North America—a breakaway that occurred after the election of Gene Robinson as bishop in the Episcopal Church. At the time of his election, Robinson was openly gay and married to another man.

My church fostered suspicion of LGBTQ people. The leaders of my church considered Jesus' call to nonviolence impractical in our current context. We were encouraged not to take certain commands in the Bible literally. Yet, I was taught an accurate reading of the Bible required people to restrict marriage to one man and one woman for life. My church believed that failure to embrace this sexual ethic was part of a larger liberal project to water down the faith by demythologizing miracles and denying the bodily resurrection. Eventually this would lead people down a path of destruction.

It was this last worry that was most compelling. We didn't hate LGBTQ people. And we didn't believe we were their enemies. Rather, we were filled with compassion for them. We wanted to release people from sinful lives bound up in physical, spiritual, and emotional harm. I worried these people would put themselves in danger of falling eternally outside the grace of God. These were concerns that kept me awake at night and fed my allegiance to the theology of my church.

But in that church context, people in the LGBTQ community were our enemies. And though I denied it then, I was theirs. We held power—economic, judicial, and ecclesial—over them. Eventually, I would have to choose. Would I be an enemy to the tradition of my youth or an enemy to people at the margins? Would I side with those who had the monopoly on church power, the center of authority for thousands of years? Or would I choose people who were bullied in school and were targets of violence? Would I side with people who supported the legal discrimination of queer people at work, or people who could not visit partners in the hospital or receive spousal benefits?

The powerful forces of compassion and empathy helped shift my perspective. But just as importantly, I learned how to assess power, how it works, and who has it. And I began to see the line in the Bible that Jesus draws between himself and the powerful. Eventually I had to make a choice. I decided I would put myself on the side of the line where I saw Jesus. I was wrong about LGBTQ people. I repent of it, and the work of my life is to undo, in whatever measure I can, these past harms.

— — —

THE NEW TESTAMENT is a collection of writing for a specific people, penned to living communities. It is a cultural product that contains within it the revelation of good news, God in flesh. The work before us is complicated; it requires discerning within Scripture where Jesus' good news is alive in history and how his message is relevant for the questions we face today. There is no plain reading of Scripture, no return to a pure text. There isn't a correct tool or translation or method that, if we found it, would provide a biblical response to every situation we face. Instead, there is the Holy Spirit, the Bible, and us.

Not all churches believe that the Bible is safe in the hands of ordinary people. There are churches who entrust the reading of Scripture to experts, where the "correct" reading of the Bible is determined by long-established power. As a young person, I couldn't see that the struggles over human sexuality and Scripture in my church were not about correct interpretation, but about the problem of power slipping away. I couldn't see what lay behind the façade of Scriptural integrity: a fear of losing control.

The book of Acts gave me hope in the messy, fumbling process of people figuring out what it means to be the church—for different and diverse people to work out their lives in the grain of God's liberating love. Acts of the Apostles is a window where we can peer into the shared life of the earliest followers of Jesus working out the politics of God's reign now absent their chief rabbi. How will they eat and make decisions, worship and think about money? How would they decide who should be in charge or how they should live in relation to their pagan neighbors? What would they believe? Who would run the soup kitchen? How would they believe it with their bodies? Who would be in charge?

In Acts we see the complexity of this Jesus-life for those who were stratified by economics, ritual, and sexual difference. The book of Acts offers no easy answers. We aren't shown a flow chart for decision-making or given a guidebook for the structure of church polity. We can't squeeze out a single interpretation of the Bible from the book of Acts. Instead, we are given the people in the room, led by the Holy Spirit, to work out what God is speaking to them. Over and over in the Gospels, Jesus explains that determining the patterns of earthly life for this reordered creation is up to people. Decisions we make here are bound in heaven itself (Matthew 18:18). In Acts, we see what that looks like.

In Acts 15 the Jewish followers of Jesus are trying to figure out what to do about the Gentiles who want to join them. At least that's what the disciples think they are doing. The truth of the matter is that the Holy Spirit is already at work among the pagans of Jerusalem, whether the disciples like it or not. Paul and Barnabas return from their work and report what they have seen—God has given the Gentiles the Holy Spirit. They wonder, what should happen next with these pagans? What should we do about them?

The disciples need to decide about circumcision, the marker of God's covenant on the bodies of male Israelites. This embodied sign sets Israel apart from all the nations of the world. It is a sign on the part of the body used for procreation, for passing down the covenant from generation to generation. This is the sign of God's covenant from the beginning. But that symbolism is not clear to everyone.

The Judeans want to keep the line, absorbing Jesus-believing Gentiles into Jewish ethnicity. It seems amiss that God would change God's mind, now working in pagan people without having their identities subsumed into Judaism. There's nothing wrong with the circumcision of Jews for the writer of Acts. Both John the Baptist and Jesus are circumcised. Paul is present when Timothy is circumcised, and Stephen mentions this ritual in his speech before he's stoned. The concern for Paul is not circumcision itself, but the role it plays as a requirement for Gentile followers of Jesus to join the movement.

And then we get a glimpse at how the early church uses Scripture. Instead of culling through the data, the early church turns to a little verse from Amos, one of the minor prophets.

They look to a prophecy that has nothing to do with circumcision, but everything to do with another refrain in the Hebrew Bible: God's intention is to bring peace to all creation. God will also envelope the Gentiles into the redeeming love that begins with an eternal covenant with Israel:

> On that day I will raise up
>   the booth of David that is fallen,
> and repair its breaches,
>   and raise up its ruins,
>   and rebuild it as in the days of old;
> in order that they may possess the remnant of Edom
>   and all the nations who are called by my name,
>   says the Lord who does this. (Amos 9:11-12)

Whenever I lead sharing time, the time we discern Scripture together as a church in Sunday worship, I use the same words: "Where have we sensed the Spirit moving among us today?" I ask because it isn't enough to read the Bible with the question "How do we think God should act?" guiding us. That's a question that eliminates God's continued work among us. Instead, we begin with an exclamation: "We have seen God at work! Let me tell you how." All of Scripture—all of our past, all of our hopes, all that we do—is interpreted through this exclamation, as we work out where we are seeing God among us, alive in our midst.

When the earliest Jewish followers of Jesus read the Bible, they looked for the places that made sense of God's work among the Gentiles. They looked for Scripture to confirm what they experienced as God's clear action.

Circumcision would not be a part of the Gentiles' transformation into the beloved community that began with God's covenant with Israel. There would be other ways the Gentiles transformed their lives. The former pagans were prohibited from eating food sacrificed to idols and consuming blood that had been strangled. These rules served a purpose. They lowered the barrier to table fellowship. The apostles looked for ways that Gentiles could eat with Jews while respecting cultural identity markers.

How could they create a new people across dividing lines—a people who would protest against the empire and against its exploitation of temple sex slaves and idolatrous worship of the emperor? They would learn to eat together. This is not sentimental choice. As we've seen, the decision to establish table fellowship was a matter of addressing social and economic disparities. It required the early church to take their divisions seriously in order to take down the scaffolding of enmity.

— — —

THE DECISION IN ACTS about Gentile inclusion gives us an opportunity to explore a complicated virtue—tolerance. Without tolerance (putting up with that which we find morally disagreeable) we dead-end in factionalism, carving out smaller and smaller niches of commonality. Perhaps more importantly, tolerance keeps violence at bay. Through my inclusion of difference I can make space for someone else's difference without meddling in it or, even worse, coercing them into taking up my position.

Tolerance, though, becomes complicated when power enters the picture. It's easy to imagine the good of tolerance between people of equal standing. As long as we are equals, we can negotiate our difference. We can live with these differences and even cultivate friendship and community even though moral differences exist between us. But this kind of scenario rarely exists in real life. If you are in a position of authority over me—if I am your child or you are my boss—then the terrain of power changes. If you withdraw your toleration, you are in position to do so without offending the terms of tolerance. After all, you are in charge.

In the stories of the early church, certain differences between the first followers of Jesus are regarded as tolerable and others intolerable. Often intolerable actions and forms of life (such as requiring circumcision of Gentiles) are deemed as such because of their bearing on the social and economic hierarchy in the church. Paul and the other apostles don't spend time in the weeds, ordering every aspect of human life in the early church. We know nothing about how people in the early church raised their children, what plays they watched, what their friendships were like with people outside the church, or how they ran their households. Significant differences existed among the people in the early church, people from different ethnicities and social classes. Paul's letters to these early churches do not require absolute conformity even around pressing moral issues. Instead, Paul jumps in with correction when social and economic power begin to divide the community, or, in Pauline language, when human practices threaten the church's oneness in Christ.

Paul's letters are often penned to communities in crisis because they have brought the hierarchies of the old order into the life of the church. These are moments when we see asymmetry between "virtuous tolerators" and "powerless recipients" warping the possibility of true communion and shared life.[3] In these letters we get a sense of what is intolerable for a diverse people whose purpose is to display God's good news for the world.

The decision over whether or not to require circumcision of Gentiles is only the beginning of disagreement and complication for the people drawn together in the new life of Jesus. Overnight, people of different ethnicities and social status are tossed together in the church. In the epistles, Paul's letters to the earliest churches, we watch as this unruly community figured out common life, difference, and how these are discerned.

The early church is rife with disagreement. There are conflicts over which leaders to follow, the presence of false teaching, power factions cropping up, and the rich lording their wealth over the poor. We learn about one of these conflicts in a letter Paul writes to the church at Corinth.

At the end of the day, laborers and slaves make their way down the streets of Corinth to a large, stately home. The sun has already set, and these laborers can feel the weariness setting in. They are the poorest of Corinth, the people who work the fields and manage the affairs of wealthy masters. A man named

Paul has told them about Jesus, who was sent from God to set right the terror of these days. Paul preached that, in Jesus, they were no longer separated by religious practice or social status.

As these poorest people in Corinth make their way to the upper room, they hear the sound of drunken laughter. The landowners and masters are already there. The smell of food is in the air, but the table is filled with empty dishes.

The workers of Corinth have arrived for a communion meal after everyone else because their labor requires them to work late into the day. By the time they arrive the wealthy, higher-class people have eaten almost all the food and are, more or less, drunk. In 1 Corinthians 11, Paul calls this group of lower-class, economically marginal people the Weak. The other group he calls the Strong.[4]

This economic division was also a class divide. In the ancient world upper-class people, not unlike today, had excess time and money. Wealthy people used that money and leisure to attend lectures and to expose themselves to new ideas. Paul has heard these upper-class people quoting the Cynic and Stoic philosophers. We can imagine them justifying their actions through phrases they've heard at lectures and in conversations with other elites: "All things are lawful for me" (1 Corinthians 6:12); "Food is meant for the stomach, and the stomach for food" (1 Corinthians 6:13); "no idol in the world really exists" (1 Corinthians 8:4).

These upper-class people are right. What they learned is true. They rightly perceive that there's nothing wrong with eating meat sacrificed to idols. The gods who are the subject of these sacrifices are worthless. Worshiping these gods is no different than worshiping an old hat or a molding loaf of bread. It's absurd and so is the idea that sacrifice to wood or stone would mean anything to the one true God of Creation.

In other words, the Strong are correct. They have good theology that gives them the freedom to eat meat sacrificed to idols, which is why it is significant that we hear what happens next. It doesn't matter that the Strong are accurate. "Knowledge puffs up, but love builds up," Paul tells the church in conflict at Corinth. "Anyone who claims to know something does not yet have the necessary knowledge; but anyone who loves God is known by him" (1 Corinthians 8:2-3). The Strong might be right, Paul tells the upper-class people of Corinth. They might have the correct interpretation of Scripture. They might have the right ideas, but that's not love. The only kind of knowledge that matters in the church is the kind that moves different people, once economic and ethnic enemies, toward a new body that is a living, active witness of God's love.

The Strong, the upper class, defend their right to continue to build social capital at pagan tables. As we've seen, these meals are the center of business dealings. So why shouldn't they continue to profit from this system? Why shouldn't they continue to work within the patron-client system to build networks and to increase their wealth? Paul reminds them that being right doesn't matter. What matters most is the flourishing of the whole body of the church, including the Weak.

The Weak, those who don't have access to the philosophical teaching of the Strong, are confused and upset as they watch their fellow church members eating pagan food and building social networks among the pagan elite. These actions by the Strong cause confusion, pain, and anguish in the Corinthian church. They cause division.

We might expect Paul to tell the Weak to get over it and get educated or tell each group to give a little and meet in the middle. After all, the Strong are correct. But, in line with the great reversals that so often happened in Jesus' life, Paul flips the matter around. The Strong are told to adjust their lives to conform to the Weak. People who have more, who got lucky to be born into wealthy families, who ended up with leisure time and money that allowed them to learn new things—these people are instructed to align their lives with lower-class people in the community.

In his letter to the Corinthian church, Paul asks the people in this community to conform their eating times and practices to workers and slaves—people who are on the far margins of power in Roman society. Paul can see that the wealthy are using their freedom in Christ, the freedom from belief in idols, to rationalize their division. But liberty isn't everything. Love is.

Paul can tell that the publicans and landowners don't take seriously the ritual significance of the Lord's Supper. "For when the time comes to eat, each of you goes ahead with your own supper, and one goes hungry and another becomes drunk," Paul blasts the Strong in his letter (1 Corinthians 11:21). The Lord's Supper brings together Jesus' followers as one body. Communion proclaims their unity across differences. "Whoever, therefore, eats the bread or drinks the cup of the Lord in an unworthy manner," Paul warns, "will be answerable for the body and blood of the Lord" (1 Corinthians 11:27). This is a significant charge. It is a judgment upon the church when the wealthy leisure class leaves the poorest in Corinth hungry. To reenact the power of social hierarchy in the unifying ritual of the church is to mock the body of Christ.

One of the most famous passages in the Bible is also found in the letter to the church of Corinth. In it we discover that love is patient and love is kind. Love does not boast, and it isn't self-seeking. When we step into the details of life among the Corinthian church, we get a better sense of what that means. It has less to do with emotion or empathy or with having the same political or economic ideology. Love takes shape in our material lives.

Paul instructs the Strong to give up meat purchased in marketplaces and to stop attending feasts dedicated to the gods. Rather than finishing the meal before the laborers arrive, the leisure class should wait for everyone to show up. Love re-orients life toward those without power. Love eliminates the structures of hierarchal authority that dominate people's lives. And it is here, when social stratification is eliminated, that a community of love can flourish.

Paul shows us that there's an even deeper freedom at work in the Christian life: a freedom beyond the impotence of idols. The people of Corinth are free to live strange lives; they are welcomed to live outside the expectations of a good life set by those at the top of the social and economic hierarchy. They are freed to become the body of Jesus, enfleshed on Earth.

— — —

BUT PAUL IS not always successful at convincing the church to change its economic and social structure for the good of the most vulnerable among them. At times, powerful people over-take the community of the church and refuse to undergo the change in socioeconomic status, cultural identity, or solidarity required for a diverse people to be one. When this happens, when a faction or a false teacher sways the congregation to-ward disunity and dissension, Paul does not demand unity at all costs. There are times when we can no longer hold together because the cost is too great.

Over the past decades in response to the damage and pain of fundamentalism, I've watched churches turn a new page of tolerance and inclusion. We may disagree, I hear in these churches, but we can worship together. We can establish relationships first; this will propel us toward one another, allowing us to overcome even the most profound and painful divisions between us. We can see the image of God in one another. Often in these churches, we hear that the focus should be on Jesus rather than on those things that divide us—race, gender, sexuality, or socioeconomic status.

But this veneer is thin, and it only requires slight pressure to reveal how little force this kind of inclusiveness can withstand. Those who bear the cost of that eventual tearing are people who occupy the margins of social and economic power—the people whose lives are not celebrated but tolerated in the church. They are the disrupters of the peaceful status quo of enemy-free church spaces. I've heard stories about this feigned peace in churches that refuse to offer a clear statement regarding their stance on LGBTQ people. Despite a clear anti-gay theological position—known and taught by church leaders—this knowledge is kept secret from the people in the pews. The decision to keep this information hidden can be a source of damage and trauma to LGBTQ people. It is not unusual for LGBTQ people to make the discovery about the church's orientation toward them only after forming deep bonds or being rejected from a leadership position when they come out.

Churches err when inclusion and tolerance mask conflict as a way to avoid the costly work of anti-oppression. Danté Stewart was in his truck when he heard the news report about Alton Sterling, a Black man shot and killed at close range by police in Baton Rouge during an attempted arrest. Sitting there, Stewart took time to compose himself. Danté, a Black man, was about to lead an anti-racism training for a predominately white church, a church he knew was more interested in forgiveness than righteous anger.

Looking back over the years he spent in evangelicalism, attempting to shift white churches away from apathy and toward racial justice, Stewart says bluntly, "The project failed."[5] "They wanted change," he writes, "but not the type of change that meant being reeducated out of their racial ignorance." Often these congregations wanted cosmetic changes, such as the cultivation of a multiracial worship service, all without discussing the structural anti-Blackness and white supremacy within their leadership and culture. "These conversations would lead to minimal action—someone would say we would be okay, then segue into saying something that would move our churches and society into 'racial reconciliation.'"[6] Rarely did Stewart see movement that addressed core issues.

Jesus draws a line and places himself on one side of it. He asks us to stand there with him. We leave behind our old lives to join him there. This means that the good news will disrupt our jobs and the way we spend money, our conceptions of racial hierarchies and church leadership, and our assumptions about policing and prisons. And these changes are not always received as good news. Reworking life toward the gospel is often labeled as disruptive and divisive by those who benefit from a social order constructed by coercive power.

Our churches are not neutral enclaves of equality. Like the church in Corinth, we replicate society's economic, social, gendered, and racial hierarchies in our congregations. We create structures where certain groups of people make decisions and control the money. Our boards, vestries, and denominations determine who has power. We are embedded in traditions that exacerbate inequality and cut off opportunities for discernment because we fear conflict and its accompanying loss of members and revenue.

As Danté Stewart experienced, it is often people at the margins of power who bear the weight of changing the culture of power in the local church. It is not unusual for people at the center of power to charge those with marginal access to power with the task of fixing their own marginalization. It is a problem when those who are the strongest advocates for tolerance are those who do not bear the weight of that tolerance. Pay attention to who is asking for unity. Bracketing off part of people's lives—as if our sexual identity, gender, or race were a secondary consideration—is only possible for people whose identity is considered normative, whole, and good in the hierarchy of social power. This kind of unity is only possible for those who have little on the line—those whose bodies are considered tolerable.

This way of organizing church life is a manifestation of the old order that Jesus comes to abolish. Inclusion can be a way to avoid difficult conversations that could change our churches at their very core. These difficult conversations could cause people to leave the church. When our congregations avoid transformative conflict because of fears of alienating people empowered by money and influence, we are in breach of the good news.

— — —

TOLERANCE OF INTOLERABLE difference is a cost born by those dispossessed of power. I've watched queer people struggle for recognition in anti-gay churches, women who spend their lives attempting to carve out priestly spaces in the Catholic church, and Black leaders burn out within the intractable white supremacy of evangelicalism. Some people are called to this work.

They cultivate communities and practices that sustain them for the long work of shifting a culture. But others are broken by it. They continue on because they are told that church is not a place for their nourishment, nor a space to hold their anger and pain, but a place to sacrifice themselves. They are present to offer the gift of diversity to people intertwined in their oppression. The terrible, death-dealing lie is that their self-destruction is required to love their enemies.

I am certain that if Jesus' news will be good, it will be good for those who have been merely tolerated in the church rather than brought to the center as its priests. And that good news comes to us through the word Jesus speaks to his disciples as they prepare to go out as witnesses to proclaim this good news.

In the gospel of Matthew, Jesus gathers seventy-two of his disciples. I can imagine the shock on their faces when, instead of receiving a packing list, Jesus instructs them to go into Judea empty-handed. The disciples will be vulnerable to the hospitality of the community they enter. And it is there that they will pronounce peace. This is not the peace of the *Pax Romana,* a peace that thrives on the suppression of discord, sedition, and war by the sword. Instead, the peace Jesus offers is communal good, wholeness, and social reordering where the first become last and last become first. It is a peace that can be offered and can be taken away.

The disciples are to come to a town and welcome the reception of whomever will take them in. But Jesus tells them something else—"If anyone will not welcome you or listen to your words, shake off the dust from your feet as you leave that house or town" (Matthew 10:14). Jesus alludes to a practice of "dusting off the feet," to symbolically shake off the dirt from Gentile lands that gathers on the sandals. It is a rejection of self-purification.

In this metaphor, those who refuse the good news are comparable to the archetypal pagan nations of the Hebrew Bible, Sodom and Gomorrah. In his pronouncement to leave behind even religious kin who will not receive the good news, Jesus shifts the disciples' allegiances. As he says throughout his teachings, the natural bonds of lineage, tradition, and practice do not constitute the kind of solidarity that interests Jesus. In the reconfigured age of good news, we discover our enemies are just as likely those with whom we share the most in common—our communities, churches, and families.

When I see hopeful change-makers broken by powerful cultures of white supremacy, homophobia, and sexism, I remember the words of Samuel Wells: "This isn't failure; it's rejection."[7] Jesus doesn't want us broken apart and martyred for people who refuse the good news of our lives. We are given permission to leave. Holding on to power, ignoring the words of prophets, refusing to hear those who have news of liberation – these are their own judgments. We have no need to give ours. In the end, ordering life by the rules of coercive power opens the door to destruction and death.

This good news will not come from the wealthy or the politically and socially connected. It will not come from those obsessed with their own righteousness through piety or religious practice. It will not come from those who lay heavy burdens on people's backs or who ignore the cries of the poor, the orphan, and the widow. To follow Jesus into the life of the beatified community requires discernment between difference and enmity. This discernment is a form of life that shifts and changes and loops back on itself—where we must fail and repent and try again. As we go about the work, we claim our place in a new order of forgiveness and grace that wears down the deep patterns of violence we each hold in our bodies.

— — —

WE CANNOT COMMIT to this life if we are unwilling to let go those who are against God's renewed order. Jesus will come among those pushed aside and pushed down, those marked as "others," those deemed suspicious because of who they love or how they live. One of the most sobering passages in Matthew comes from a long teaching about future judgment. Jesus tells the listeners that a time will come when peoples are divided like sheep and goats. One group will be blessed, one cast out.

But the criteria for this decision are notably absent of beliefs or doctrines. No confession of faith, no baptism, and no heresy mark the difference between those who are judged in this apocalyptic story. Instead, God welcomes those who saw Jesus in the hungry, the thirsty, the stranger, the naked, the sick, and the imprisoned. And it is the righteous, those welcomed into the kingdom, who are left puzzled. They ask, "When was it that we saw you hungry and gave you food, or thirsty and gave you something to drink? And when was it that we saw you a stranger and welcomed you, or naked and gave you clothing? And when was it that we saw you sick or in prison and visited you?" (Matthew 25:37-39). Even as they did these things, they did not know that they had cared for God. They attended to the places of suffering they saw around them, and there God was present.

From this passage we learn that there is enough evidence in the suffering of the world for people to encounter and love Jesus. We should not need miraculous visitations or stirring teachings. There is enough suffering in the world that people do not need to be convinced to align their lives with those who are victims in the old order of power. We won't get this right every time, and the way toward unity around the crucified and risen Jesus is often marked with failure and repentance.

This is where Jesus draws the line—where he invites us to set up our lives and welcome others to the liberatory and disruptive good news of upended social convention. This is where a new people is made from those who were hungry and thirsty, who waste away in prisons, and who linger in sick wards. Jesus cares about what we do with our lives. If there are people who will not join this work, who harm the witness of this good news, we shake the dust and return to the work given us to do.

–TEN–

Becoming Enemies to Mammon

THERE ARE PLACES throughout the Bible that help us in the work of realigning our lives with that of Jesus. In the New Testament, enmity has a program and a logic. The old order—a social order designed for Miss Faye to die in prison and that locked Ann Atwater and C.P. Ellis in a retributive struggle—spread its roots through the world in a form called Mammon.

In the Gospels, Jesus presents his disciples with a choice. "No one can serve two masters; for a slave will either hate the one and love the other, or be devoted to one and despise the other. You cannot serve God and wealth (Mammon)" (Matthew 6:24). To worship God, we must first become an enemy to Mammon.

Mammon is not only wealth in the form of coin or cash. It is wealth as a source of power that controls our access to everything. In order to secure access to material and immaterial goods we are taught we must put our faith in wealth's ability to work on our behalf. Mammon is totalizing because it assigns everything a value. It creates competition for a place within a hierarchy of winners and losers. To prosper from Mammon is to offer Mammon our worship.

The church has often taught that we can consciously lay down our allegiance to Mammon by retraining our desires. Jesus' concern, this reading goes, is a matter of one's orientation toward money. One way to justify keeping excessive wealth is to claim that the real problem is desire. Do I want wealth and its trappings more than I desire God? As long as I am not greedy, and as long as I control my desire, I can worship God rightly despite my place in the economic order.

The New Testament has different interests. Jesus names Mammon as a force of exploitation perpetuated by tax collectors and publicans to enrich the Romans on the backs of the common Judean people. Participation in this economy excludes worship of God because it demands a life built around and for the structure of Mammon. For Jesus it is not a matter of how we use our wealth but of wealth itself.

This crystalizes in Jesus' encounter with a wealthy young man who comes to Jesus asking what he must do to "inherit eternal life" (Luke 18:18). The young man explains that he has kept all the laws of Moses—on its own, a remarkable feat. Jesus goes on to explain that there is something the young man is missing: "Sell all that you own and distribute the money to the poor, and you will have treasure in heaven; then come, follow me" (Luke 18:22). Getting rid of wealth is the way the young man will cease worship of Mammon; this is the precondition to becoming a follower of Jesus.

Jesus does not demand generosity or charitable giving. Jesus does not ask for a reorientation toward wealth or for the young man to keep his money and continue to use it for good. Jesus is uninterested in internal motivations or declarations of faith unless they are matched by our lives. He tells the rich young man to choose worship by virtue of ridding himself of his wealth. The rich young man walks away sad, for he had many possessions. This story is not aberration. It is an invitation consistent throughout the New Testament, an invitation that continues to invite us to lay down our worship of Mammon.

— — —

ON MAY 4, 1969, the organ at Riverside Church began to play as James Forman made his way down the aisle to the front of the sanctuary. He had come to demand $500 million. The pastor of Riverside instructed the organist to play loud enough to drown out Forman's request.[1]

Forman was involved in both the Student Non-Violent Coordinating Committee (SNCC) and the Black Panther Party, but it was his work with the National Black Economic Development Conference (NBEDC) that led him to Riverside on that day. He came bearing his Black Manifesto. "For centuries we have been forced to live as colonized people in the United States," wrote the authors, "victimized by the most vicious, racist system in the world. . . . We are therefore demanding that white Christian churches and Jewish synagogues which are part and parcel of the system of capitalism, that they begin to pay reparations to black people in this country."[2] Forman had come to Riverside Church that day to ask for its contribution.

The NBEDC wanted the money to buy land and establish Black-owned farms, to create a publishing industry for national news that could compete with the white establishment press, and to found a Black-run university in the South. The request was not for a donation to charities. NBEDC had a broader vision for institutional shifts that would renew a Black economy and change the trajectory for generational opportunities for the Black community. Without comprehensive restructuring of economic opportunity, the racial wealth and opportunity gap would continue to widen.

The Black Manifesto caused an uproar in white churches around the country, including in my tradition, the Mennonite church. A few months after Forman's demand, on August 16, 1969, Black Mennonite pastor John Powell entered the (Old) Mennonite Church General Assembly in Turner, Oregon, to issue the same call Forman brought to Riverside. He wanted the church to establish a fund in the amount of $500,000 "for the purpose of developing and expanding ways of serving the urban poor and other minorities in new and meaningful ways," and for anti-racism training in white churches.[3]

The denomination managed to raise no more than $100,000. Riverside gave Forman a fraction of the $500 million in the form of donations to Black nonprofits.

— — —

MAKING REPARATIONS is an economic reckoning and one way to follow Jesus in uprooting worship of Mammon. Offering reparations to the descendants of enslaved Africans is a way for the white supremacist government of the United States to publicly acknowledge and repair its generational theft of Black wealth and opportunity. We can trace this theft back to an American economy and country built by the labor of enslaved Africans brought to the United States through the Middle Passage.

For centuries after slavery, the United States government broke promises to Black citizens, including the Reconstruction plan of "forty acres and a mule," redlining, racialized restrictions on the G.I. bill, environmental racism, and the unchallenged persistence of a wage gap. With each generation, the economic disenfranchisement of the Black community is compounded, the rift widening. Reparation is a form of leveling and repairing the economic disparities intentionally created to sustain a racial category called whiteness.

Charitable giving based on the personal preferences of those who have benefited from the economic systems of whiteness will not achieve Jesus' mission of redemption. As we've seen throughout this book, Jesus does not wish to move around the pieces on the chess board of hierarchy, power, and privilege. He wants to topple the game altogether, putting an end to an order in which some thrive on the violence and destruction of others.

Anti-racism work that contributes to this good news moves beyond self-assessment or empathic personal relationships to the disassembling of racialized economic systems. It is not enough to enact meager cosmetic changes or to challenge a particular mindset. When we do this we turn the material reality of our faith into ideology. This is often at work when people critique the Black Lives Matter platform, and its attention to the way capitalism underpins oppression. Both conservatives and liberals are cautious to connect racism and capitalism. Conservatives often reject BLM out of hand. Liberals and progressives, by contrast, make an amorphous claim that "Black lives matter" without being willing to embrace the economic roots of racism in the United States. What they mean is "Black lives matter as long as they don't change the economic systems on which I depend for my flourishing."

Often the church prefers anti-racism that can "engender forms of white self-consciousness that can allow for more lubricated social relations," not the kind that calls into question market forces, free trade, or private property rights.[4] Racism does and will continue to thrive as long as we reduce its power to interpersonal or policy changes. Racism is insidious and pervasive because it cannot be rooted out without clearing the old systems of racial capital. The U.S. economy is based on racial capital, rooted in white people's gaining social and economic value from the lives of people of color. This nation grows in the soil tilled by Africans and African descendants, whose bodies were property.

I am grateful for white attention to microaggressions, to diverse corporate and nonprofit boards, and to church spaces absent racist tropes and stereotypes. I am grateful for robust multiculturalism centered on people of color. These are good and right forms of life. Yet they cannot come at the expense of attention to the ways that Mammon is the operational form of racism in our social order. This theft, what we call capitalism, is incompatible with our worship of God. We cannot choose both. We cannot continue with ideological changes that shift the chess pieces around without asking how we stop playing the game altogether.

In his stunning essay, "The Case for Reparations," Ta-Nehisi Coates shows the force of economic racism in the life of Clyde Ross, born into 1920s Jim Crow Mississippi. Economic forces of racism shaped his whole life.[5] Ross grew up in normalized state robbery—his family were sharecroppers locked into a system of destitution. The landowner took out the price of tools and materials from the family's expected profits as an advance. If crops failed or yield was bad, this loss was converted to debt.

Sharecropping created a social order driven by this debt, which often ended in forced labor in penal camps.

Ross's life is a case study in theft economy. When Ross was a boy, his father, unable to read and without a lawyer, was presented with a bill for $3,000 in back taxes. Because they couldn't pay, their land was seized. The losses grew. Later Ross was drafted into the Army. After his tour, he migrated to Chicago, married, and had children. But the economy of theft persisted in the North. With few other options available, Ross signed a predatory housing agreement in which the seller kept the deed of the house until the mortgage was paid. Because of this, Ross would acquire no equity on the home.

"When I found myself caught up in it, I said, 'How? I just left this mess. I just left no laws. And no regard,'" Ross told Coates in an interview. Like many Black people, Ross fought back, joining the Contract Buyers League. The League demanded payback on contracts, structural improvements, and a change to the rental price structure. Assessing the work of the League, Coates remarks, "They were no longer fleeing in hopes of a better deal elsewhere. They were charging society with a crime against their community. They wanted the crime publicly ruled as such. . . . They were seeking reparations."

— — —

REPARATIONS MOVE US from giving charitably to tackling the roots of economic injustice in the United States. It is not enough to give away a bit of what we have. Instead, the economy of the reign of God will offer a revision of the way wealth, consumption, and accumulation act in our lives. This is the way we restructure the deception of scarcity that divides us and creates the conditions for enmity.

The ancient world in which the Gospels were written was also a time of vast economic exploitation. Ancient Rome, like the United States, created a system with an immense chasm between the "haves" and "have-nots." Entering this context, Jesus intended to upend and reinterpret social practices that were the backbone of Mammon. From time to time Jesus offers teachings about charity, but the collective resonance of the Gospels is economic disruption.

The larger vision for a renewed order of creation includes this social reorder. As we've seen throughout this book, Jesus does not come to Earth to create new victims. He also does not look to engender new poverties. The new order is an inverse of socioeconomic hierarchies in which some flourish while others perish. Many of these upheavals happen around tables. Because meals are the place where social contracts are made and where client-patron relationships are established, it is significant that Jesus takes the risk of being subsumed into social allegiance with dishonest people—"sinners." He takes on a bad reputation. He has no regard for this social hierarchy in which he is embedded.

One day Jesus is invited to eat at the home of Simon the Pharisee (Luke 7:36-50). Jesus is greeted with an extravagant meal, the kind of meal that could not be reciprocated by the wandering peasant (Jesus) who is the guest of honor. Simon's hospitality is not a matter of kindness. Simon has brought Jesus there, writes Philip Goodchild, to bring Jesus under his patronage. By establishing this social contract, Jesus will owe Simon something for the honor of coming under Simon's household. Jesus will be "obliged to offer favours and services to his benefactor."[6] We are witnessing a business meeting. But then the meal is interrupted.

Into this all-male gathering comes a woman—"a sinner"—with no reputation and nothing to lose. The woman uses her hair to wipe the feet of Jesus. She weeps and kisses the feet of the honored guest. The host is embarrassed to have a person of such low social status enter the meal-as-business-meeting and display such inappropriate behavior.

Just as in the meal with the tax collectors, Jesus appears to accept the actions of a person who would be considered debasing company. This is the beginning of Jesus' reputation in Luke for being a friend of tax collectors and sinners. Instead of condemning the woman, writes Goodchild, Jesus tells a story about two people who owe debts. In this metaphor Jesus compares Simon and the woman, putting them in the same category. Two people owe debts. Simon is unnerved. His wealth puts him at a different social rank, and Jesus has no business juxtaposing him with this woman. In dismissing this economic and social hierarchy, Jesus excises the social component. He compares the two people before him using "a radical simplification of obligation to a single monetary scale."[7]

In other words, Jesus treats Simon and the woman as equals, each owing a debt. The woman owes a larger debt than Simon, who does quite well at keeping up his legal obligations. But when the debt is canceled the one who will love the debt-forgiver more is the one who owed more. She is the one who truly loves, not to secure Jesus' patronage but out of desire and longing. In one of the great biblical reversals, we learn that she is the hospitable one, not Simon. Of the woman "no further services are required," writes Goodchild.[8] Jesus doesn't use this as a moment to flip the script, to bring the woman into patronage of Jesus. Instead, Jesus frees her from obligation. Her debt is forgiven and she owes him nothing.

- - -

JESUS TELLS ANOTHER STORY about how the worship of Mammon can result in the destruction of human community. In this story, there is a rich man who eats well and dresses in fine clothes. And there is a beggar named Lazarus, covered in sores, who sits at the rich man's door and longs for scraps from his table:

> The poor man died and was carried away by the angels to be with Abraham. The rich man also died and was buried. In Hades, where he was being tormented, he looked up and saw Abraham far away with Lazarus by his side. He called out, "Father Abraham, have mercy on me, and send Lazarus to dip the tip of his finger in water and cool my tongue; for I am in agony in these flames." But Abraham said, "Child, remember that during your lifetime you received your good things, and Lazarus in like manner evil things; but now he is comforted here, and you are in agony." (Luke 16:22-25)

Blame doesn't befall the rich man because he did not share what he had. The problem is not his lack of generosity, or that he did not cultivate good desires. He failed because he received good things during his lifetime while Lazarus received nothing. The reality of the charge should challenge readers because, at the end of the day, the eternal fate of Lazarus and the rich man have nothing to do with belief, piety, religious identity, or the proclamation "Jesus is Lord." The only consideration is their money. One has it and one does not.

This stunning conclusion is less remarkable when we remember Jesus forces a choice between two masters, two forms of logic, and two operational systems: the reign of God or Mammon. We cannot service both; we will love one and hate the other. Money itself causes the problems for the rich man. He has accepted the terms of a master and is bound to that master's service. The rich man's hoarding of wealth is part of a larger system of economic exploitation. Judea, as was saw in an earlier chapter, was a state of dramatic economic stratification that relied upon predation of the poorest and vulnerable. There is no separating wealth from how it is earned.

"Assimilation into the Roman Empire," writes Philip Goodchild, "had turned Judea and Galilee into effective tax farms or private estates, a patchwork of households where the pursuit of unlimited production was the primary goal."[9] The ancient taxation system of Rome was not designed to gather resources for redistribution for the common good of the people. Instead, taxing was the method by which occupying Rome squeezed money out of already destitute common people.

The power of the Herodian puppet government over Judea came from its ability to siphon money from laborers through a severe taxation system. Because Rome controlled currency, it dictated how money was used and moved. Money came from Rome. It carried the picture of Caesar's face. This money eventually returned to Caesar. By definition, "to accumulate wealth," writes Goodman, "was to participate in a system of exploitation and extortion."[10]

This is no less true today. There is, as the unattributed saying goes, no ethical spending under capitalism. Despite our attention to fair trade or conscientious shopping, there is no extracting ourselves in total from the exploitation of labor, global systems of corporate theft, or corporations' control of nations. And so, for those of us who worship Jesus, there is no "outside," no pure retreat from the world of the rich man—for any of us. And while there is something in this story about ostentatious wealth being obscene in light of the crushing poverty that so many endure, Jesus' life complicates the matter.

Jesus, while owning little (he appears to hold no property, shares a common purse with the disciples, and depends on hospitality for survival), is often seen enjoying rich meals and accepting showy gifts like an expensive perfume poured out on his feet. The first miracle at Cana is one of excess. When the wine runs out Jesus produces hundreds of gallons more of an even better vintage than what was served before the guests became drunk off the original, inferior batch. In the wilderness he breaks bread, creating excess once again, enough to fill twelve baskets (Mark 6:43).

Jesus' intention for the new order of God's reign is not to universalize poverty through asceticism (the only way to more or less extract one's self from economic exploitation). Perhaps because Jesus' teachings are so severe, it isn't unusual for people to be pulled into an ethical nihilism in light of the all-encompassing power of Mammon that shapes our world. Often this comes in the form of relativizing wealth on a global scale, reducing our ability to act ethically to personal choice. An example of this is the World Wealth Calculator, a tool that allows people to punch in their yearly salary and see their global ranking in wealth. I, for example, am somewhere in the richest 10 percent of the world. The purpose of the calculator is to help people understand of the enormity of global poverty. But frequently this tool is used to relativize the categories of wealth. The difference between someone earing $40,000 a year and someone earning $200,000 a year is negligible when some people earn around $1 a day. Someone barely getting by in the United States is "rich" in a global order.

This is useful information in one sense and problematic in another. There is also, according to the World Wealth Calculator, a small percentage difference between me and Jeff Bezos, who, as I write these words, is on the cusp of becoming the world's first trillionaire, a leap in wealth made from exploiting the devastation of the global pandemic. Bezos, the founder and primary shareholder of Amazon, has hoarded a vast amount of the world's wealth by building an empire at considerable human and environmental cost. At the same time, someone who makes the U.S. minimum wage, currently a jaw-dropping $7.25 an hour, is nineteen times wealthier than a billion people in the world.

Both of these realities can be true. But the global scale of poverty can lead us to define "rich" and "poor" according to bank account amounts rather than the way Mammon shapes our social order. It can also become an act of self-soothing: if we in the United States are all rich compared to someone who makes a couple dollars a week, we are all at least in the same boat. Saying "We are all wealthy compared to someone else" dead-ends in inaction.

The closest "out" from Mammon's grasp is to live in poverty. But asceticism does little to right the brokenness of our world under the power of Mammon. While asceticism provides a way for us to claim purity from the taint of wealth, it does not allow participation in a graced world. Instead of austerity, writes Hollis Phelps, "The kingdom of heaven is a kingdom of excess, one that makes itself known over and above mere needs and the logic of means and ends."[11] It is an order unrestrained by scarcity.

Phelps points us away from consumption as the source of Jesus' critique and toward the problem of accumulation in the

New Testament. Because we operate within an economics designed for accumulation there is no cap to what is "enough." As Don Draper, the sage of capitalist desires, proclaims in the television show *Mad Men,* "Happiness is the moment before you want more happiness." This is the way "capitalism organizes and controls life."[12] There is no end to our desire for more, no mechanism that will shut off when we have what we need.

As it was in the ancient world, so it is today—we gain more wealth through competition for resources. Accumulating wealth differentiates us from one another, just as the rich man in Hades was separated by a great chasm from Lazarus. This separation comes into focus only after death for the rich man and Lazarus, but it is an extension of their lives on Earth. The rich man's ethic of accumulation feeds off the myth of scarcity —that one must get what one can because there is only so much to go around. Protecting ourselves against the possibility of scarcity in the future impoverishes others in the process. By contrast, refusing to hoard wealth actually distributes among us all that we need and more.

— — —

MAKING REPARATIONS is one way we address the accumulation of white wealth built through the labor of enslaved Africans and the catastrophic disenfranchisement of their Black descendants. But there are other ways we can begin to alter the structure of Mammon that creates and sustains enmity.

On Mother's Day, I brought cupcakes and balloons to the picnic shelter of a downtown park. There Southerners on New Ground threw a party for the women who had been released from jail through the bail money the community raised to free them. We sang songs in a shower of streamers. Each of the women was given a bouquet of flowers while we worked out ways to address their needs for housing, financial support, childcare, and transportation.

Each year, Southerners on New Ground organizes to free Black women from the Durham County Jail as part of a national Black Mama's Bail Out. In the United States, if a person is charged with a crime and can't pay the judge's bail, she is put in a cell. Someone can owe as little as $500 for accumulated speeding tickets, but if he cannot pay, he will wait in jail until his court date. This person is separated from family and unable to prepare a defense. Without a safety net, she is likely to lose her job, her home, and custody of her children. Hundreds of the thousands of people are in jail right now for no other reason than that they cannot afford not to be.

Bail is a system that makes money off of imprisoning human beings. Southerners on New Ground wasn't going to wait around anymore while Black women sat in cages. They weren't going to wait for laws to change or for politicians to come to their senses. They raised money and they got their people out. This action is part of a larger strategy to put an end to the carceral system in the United States, a system that largely targets people who are economic victims of racism. We know well that wealthy white people are adept at getting out of serving time not because they are less guilty or commit crimes at lower levels but because they have the financial resources to manipulate the system. Eliminating bail is one step in the broader action to end the powerful, racist, monied carceral system of the United States.

Becoming enemies to Mammon means taking up a life that recognizes how wealth is built and maintained through exploitation. The lie of scarcity leads us to believe that we need to hoard our money. Mammon whispers that there isn't enough to go around. The beatified community, with its sloshing jugs of wine, overflowing baskets of bread, and brimming vats of fish, tells a different story. Creation has everything we need if we begin with the conviction that there is enough.

ELEVEN

Whiteness and the Enemy

IT IS IMPOSSIBLE to parse out the enemies made by Mammon from the forms of white supremacy that shape and order the United States. As we come to this chapter on whiteness, I recognize that each of us participates in genealogies not of our making. We inherit bodies that draw us into the operational centers of the principalities and powers of our age. In this chapter I want to shift toward the enemy of whiteness, the history in which my body participates, and the principality that tempts my betrayal of the reign of God.

I enter this chapter cautiously because I recognize the pervasive power of whiteness. It entrenches itself in both ignorance and obsession, two forms of essentializing and over-determining of race. Whiteness reiterates its power through white people's failure to name it as a racial category and interrogate that category both as it works on history and within the lives of white people. "Whiteness," Chanequa Walker-Barnes writes, "was created as a way of determining who got to partake of the benefits of White Supremacy."[1] White bodies are elusive bodies.

Whiteness as a subject of study also runs the risk of rendering whiteness essential.[2] Sara Ahmed reminds us that whiteness is habitual to those who operate from within whiteness. "Whiteness is only invisible for those who inhabit it, or those who get so used to its inhabitance that they learn not to see it, even when they are not it." The anti-racism of white people who work and write from within whiteness can become a navel-gazing obsession with our own reflection as we stare endlessly into the mirror of our own racial performance. And so it is both risk and requirement to engage whiteness.

Because I write from the inside, I depend on others outside of whiteness to name what I see in the mirror. When the enemy is within, you need others—for me, people like Willie Jennings—to help you understand what you see. Whiteness is something that emanates both from my life as a descendent of colonizing settlers and from ancestors who benefited from a country built on the labor of enslaved Africa people and their descendants. These are forces that work upon me. Willie Jennings evokes the letter to the Ephesians—when Paul describes how our struggles are not against people but against spiritual forces—when he writes, "We have now reached a point where we can name what has not been adequately named, and that is whiteness as a principality."[3] He goes on:

> Whiteness is not the equal and opposite of blackness. It is not one racial flavor next to others. Whiteness is a way of imagining the world moving around you, flowing around

your body with you being at the center. Whiteness is a way of imagining the true, the good, and the beautiful configured around white bodies. Whiteness is a way of imagining oneself as the central facilitating reality of the world, the reality that makes sense of the world, that interprets, organizes, and narrates the world, and whiteness is having the power to realize and sustain that imagination.[4]

For Jennings, "whiteness is not a given" but a domain and a lordship.

Jennings is not the only Black intellectual to write about whiteness in this way. For Walker-Barnes, whiteness is determined by proximity or distance from Blackness as a way of constructing a sociocultural identity. It subsumes certain (non-white) bodies in order to construct power over others; this whiteness creates anti-Black economies, politics, institutions, and Christianities. "Whiteness," writes Walker-Barnes "is not just something that people possess," as if we can choose to lay it down or give it away. Instead, "it possesses them."[5] Whiteness possesses white people.

— — —

I'VE WRITTEN ABOUT how Jesus reshapes expected and naturalized categories of enemies. Jesus overcomes national and ethnic barriers and reveals that the true enemy is the person who stands against the reign of God. In order to overcome this enmity, we are called to leave behind our participation in the socioeconomic order of coercion and violence. In the Bible there is an enemy behind all of this: an enemy to whom control over the old order has been granted and to whom the Bible traces the first fatal incursion into the peaceable kingdom that leads to the reign of sin and death. This enemy goes by the name of Satan or the devil.

Whiteness as possession, as the old order under the sway of Satan, isn't an excuse to displace responsibility or a way to elicit sympathy for white people. In popular imagination possession means losing control and being outside one's self or having the self replaced by an evil spirit. At times in the New Testament demons speak for an individual, "taking them over," as it were. But the New Testament offers other accounts of possession. In the New Testament we also witness Satan's rule as ownership (however temporary) over creation and how he incites human beings to participate in this deception.

The possession of Satan is a layered deception. To be possessed is to be owned, to be bound to a system—its labor, economics, logic, and inner workings. There is no escaping the subjugation of the lord without escaping the system. Everything is absorbed in its logic—where you live, what you eat, how you survive, the shape of your family, and the outcome of future generations. You are controlled. In the United States, this logic is race, the order that enfolds within it all institutions, relationships, structures, and governances.

But in the New Testament these principalities are failed and defeated. The battle between Satan and God is not a war between equals. We do not wonder what the outcome will be. Satan's power is conditional and provisional. It is definitionally a self-deception. To believe in the domination granted by the principality and power of Satan is to be possessed by a doomed lie.

— — —

IN THE GOSPEL OF MARK we watch as Peter is pulled back into the old order of satanic domination that grips the created order. We see him possessed by it. This story occurs just after Jesus praises Peter for naming in public who Jesus is—not only a prophet but the Messiah. Peter's announcement anticipates an anointed king, one who will come to free Israel from the oppression of their Roman occupiers.

Nothing in Jesus' life so far gives Peter any reason to expect that Jesus will come to overthrow Rome. Jesus has made no claim that he will usher in a new political order. Peter says this in faith, in trust. It is a good and right hope that people will be freed from tyranny and oppression. When Jesus praises Peter for rightly naming him the expected Messiah, we recognize that Jesus' mission will bring about more than personal redemption. It will imbue creation with messianic renewal.

Peter's hopes are dashed. Jesus tells the disciples, "The Son of Man must undergo great suffering, and be rejected by the elders, the chief priests, and the scribes, and be killed, and after three days rise again" (Mark 8:31). Peter pulls Jesus aside to rebuke him. This cannot be, he thinks. There is no room in Peter's imagination for a Jesus who will cut to the very source of death itself—overcoming Satan's power over Earth. Jesus turns to the disciples so they can all hear what is about to transpire. As a lesson he says to Peter—"Get behind me, Satan! For you are setting your mind not on divine things but on human things" (Mark 8:33).

The writer of Mark describes the work of the disciples as an invasion into the territory of Satan's rulership. Jesus binds this old power—"as he and his disciples preach, heal, and cast out demons, they are plundering Satan's kingdom and setting captives free."[6] Satan's rulership of creation is restricted by Jesus.

Jesus initiates destruction to that old order from the inside, entering into the system and taking away the power of the enemy.

But Peter is drawn back into the old logic of domination and dominion. He can't see beyond the structured violence of Rome. He cannot imagine beyond endless cycles of revolutionary upheaval that replace old tyrants with new tyrannies. Jesus forcefully disabuses Peter of this future. God's reign will not be like this. The principality does not need a new master. The system itself must be destroyed.

— — —

IF WE BELIEVE, with Fannie Lou Hamer, that "nobody's free until everybody's free," then whiteness is a corruption that takes hold of people, placing them under the power of a satanic order of systemic violence and degradation. Perpetrators, victims, and survivors of the logic of race invalidate the possibility of human flourishing. Whiteness is bad for Black people. It is bad for Indigenous peoples and immigrants, for Latinx and Asian people. And whiteness is bad for white people.

"Whiteness," Chanequa Walker-Barnes reminds us, "in all its variations, is an evil ideology that relies upon brute power to enforce and maintain itself."[7] Whiteness shaped the world through enslavement, colonization, theft of land, and the genocide of Indigenous people.

One of the most gruesome and horrific forms that violence took was lynching. Lynching, an act of white supremacy, is a legacy of slavery and a shape-shifting demon of whiteness. Once lawmakers abolished slavery, the primary tool of Black oppression, white people utilized public murder, torture, dismemberment, and burning to maintain the order of white supremacy. These forms of policing Black bodies were extrajudicial only in a strictly legal sense. In reality, this was a state-sponsored form of terror to force the Black community into submission. Lynching was an institutional act often aided and abetted by the police, elected officials, and jailers.

The legal scholar Sherrilyn Ifill describes lynching not just as individual terror but as communal trauma.[8] The specter of lynching traumatized Black communities who lived under constant threat of a gruesome death for the crime of being alive and participating in public life. White mobs lynched Black men and boys over accusations of whistling or even glancing at white women. It was not unusual for white people to consider consensual relationships between Black and white people as a catalyst for a lynching. White mobs hunted down Black children and Black women. Other Black people were lynched because they stood up to economic exploitation by white businesses and landowners.

In 1918 a white mob lynched a Black man from my county named George Taylor. Taylor was accused of accosting a white farmer's wife while she was home alone with her newborn child. On the way to the county courthouse, the police handed Taylor over to a group of hooded white men. Over the course of the day, a crowd of over three hundred people gathered to participate in the lynching. Communication networks across the county told people to descend upon the ravine where Taylor was held. For Black communities, writes James Cone, an unspeakable crime like this "is so painful that they, too, try to keep these horrors buried deep down in the consciousness, until, like a dormant volcano, they erupt uncontrollably, causing profound agony and pain."[9]

Ifill describes lynching as destructive both for Black communities and for generations of white people who witnessed or accepted lynchings in their communities. Passive spectators played a key role in lynching, "observing without protest the acts of murder and torture."[10] Social scientists who study genocide and mass participation in crimes against humanity explain that "participation in collective violence leaves perpetrators with their own dangerous and persistent damage."[11] This includes defense mechanisms such as the inability to empathize with victims, which can lead to targeting other victims.

Ifill also points to the socialization of white children, who were both victims and perpetrators of lynchings. White children, some as young as ten years old, were compelled to participate in lynchings by family members. White children reenacted this violence on Black neighbor children, propagating generational racial resentment. Ifill writes that "the complicity of hundreds of thousands of whites in lynchings continues to generate profound uncertainty among Blacks about forging alliances with whites."[12] Bryan Stevenson adds, "We cannot heal the deep wounds inflicted during the era of racial terrorism until we tell the truth about it."[13]

Ifill's book inspired the nonprofit that Stevenson directs, the Equal Justice Initiative (EJI), to create a memorial to lynching victims across the country. Building on the work of the historian and activist Ida B. Wells-Barnett, EJI undertook a multiyear project to identify the victims of lynching for a certain period of U.S. history. While the named victims do not represent the breadth of victims of racial terror in the United States, the resulting Peace and Justice Memorial is the first in the United States to comprehensively memorialize the racial terror of lynching.

But most places in the United States have not yet engaged in the work of attending to communal trauma and the enmity of whiteness that forms the social order of the United States.

Instead, the trauma of lynching, slavery, police shootings, and incarceration is pushed out of sight, sunk deep into a racialized psyche. Unlike countries like Germany, Rwanda, and South Africa, the United States has not named, repented, and paid reparation for the past that shapes our current reality. We refuse to remember.

— — —

RACIALIZED VIOLENCE extends beyond a binary of victims and perpetrators as it reinforces the power of whiteness in an integrated, all-encompassing system. To be possessed within this system is to be held captive to destruction. The promise of whiteness is that people who are accepted into the category of whiteness end up on top in the racial hierarchy and therefore benefit from whiteness. But this is an incomplete picture. Whiteness requires the betrayal of ancestry and cultures of those who strive to be subsumed into whiteness. Whiteness demands everything. It is to give one's self fully over to a deception and to a Deceiver.

W.E.B. Du Bois describes this as the "political success of the doctrine of racial separation" that follows in the wake of Reconstruction.[14] During this period post–Civil War, farmers of European descent were paid a lower wage for their labor but, to make up the difference, were given the social status of whiteness as a nonmonetary form of compensation. Even as newly minted white workers, they continued to be exploited by their white bosses; but the "public and psychological wage" not to be Black was valuable enough to hold them within the system. This wage stabilized an economics of cross-racial worker exploitation. This strategy of dividing labor interests extends back to the Jamestown settlement, which designed laws to pit

European indentured servants against enslaved Africans in attempts at escaping to freedom together.

Du Bois helps us understand how the satanic power of belonging to whiteness explains how white people continue to support Donald Trump, even though the former president's policies negatively impacted all working people, including poor white people. The psychological wage of whiteness helps us understand how poor white people who need health insurance demand an end to the Affordable Care Act. It offers insight into how white family members of white men killed by gun suicide, the primary victims of gun death, refuse to demand safer gun laws. His theory helps us understand how rural white people support policies and candidates who degrade the environment even as their land and bodies are poisoned by toxic waste, hog waste pits, and fracking.[15]

But Du Bois goes further, pushing us into new territory, into a space that connects us back to the New Testament's contention that there is more than materialism at work in whiteness. There is a power binding the Earth that takes the form of rulership and desire for dominance over creation. This is the true power of whiteness. His essay "Darkwater" begins with these haunting words:

> I ask soberly:
> "But what on earth is whiteness that one should so desire
> it?" Then always, somehow, someway, I am given to understand that whiteness is the ownership of the earth, forever
> and ever, Amen![16]

"Whiteness," writes Ella Myers, "entails 'passionate' belief in one's right to everything and anything."[17] Whiteness cannot be calculated rationally. Calculable gains cannot account for the sadism and cruelty of white destruction, mutilation, and humiliation of Black bodies, including the bodies of Black children, in acts such as lynching. Instead, Du Bois's theory of hidden wage extends to whiteness as a fantasy of dominion. We can't describe whiteness merely in economic terms. We cannot assess the power of whiteness solely in terms of a calculated benefit for the progeny of people who take on whiteness, who anticipate a generational shift toward the financial well-being and social status of whiteness. There is something more sinister and powerful at work. Whiteness is religious. It demands worshipers and sacrifices.

"The present attitude of the white world is not based solely upon rational, deliberate intent," writes Du Bois. "It is a matter of conditioned reflexes; of long followed habits, customs, and folkways; of the unconscious trains of reasoning and unconscious nervous reflexes."[18] Du Bois helps us see a dogmatic belief in mastery and ownership over the world at work in whiteness. We are not simply witnessing poor people trying to get a leg up in a punishing economic climate. Regardless of one's social position, whiteness provides access to an unconscious desire for mastery of the world through the domination and destruction of Black people.

In the Gospels, the temptation of Jesus by Satan and the rebuke of Peter name the same outcome—the world handed over for domination. The possessed become the possessors, tricked into believing they can do with the created order what they will. Whiteness reenacts the original lie of the serpent in the garden—you are god unto yourself. This lie extends beyond people, beyond the subjugation of Black and brown people, poisoning Earth itself. Willie Jennings writes that race emerges from the colonial desire for mastery of the land. Colonial settlers become white at the same time that they claim the lands they encounter. Whiteness and possession are one and the same. Rather than letting the land and its peoples act upon them—as an exchange between people equally gifted with creation—Europeans become masters and possessors.[19]

— — —

WHITE DOMINATION is not confined to the past and slavery. We live with the destruction of race as possession now. My friend Rev. Jemonde Taylor labors against the forces of white supremacy in his vocation as an Episcopal priest among the people of southeast Raleigh.

"They moved our church to a dumping ground," he tells me. The story of Saint Ambrose Episcopal Church begins in the 1880s. It is one of the oldest historically Black churches in Raleigh, built after the Civil War for ministry to and with recently emancipated enslaved people of African descent. That same decade, the city of Raleigh began dumping raw sewage directly into Crabtree and Walnut Creeks that flow into Rochester Heights. Working off the theory that waste water only needed to travel fifty feet before it became potable, the city spent decades pouring sewage into the creek's estuaries, a practice that continued into the 1950s.

During the Jim Crow era in the South, policy and affordability forced Black families to locate their homes in the Walnut Creek floodplains in Rochester Heights. In 1965 workers picked up Saint Ambrose—off its foundation and onto a cart—and moved it from downtown, above the flood plain, to the sewage dump of Darby Street. That neighborhood collected sewage and waste poured into the creeks by the city. The city had been dumping sewage into Walnut Creek—in a Black neighborhood—for sixty or seventy years, Rev. Taylor reminds me.

As time went on and pollution gathered, the wetland became less and less effective at absorbing water. When even a small stormfront comes through Raleigh, land and homes and businesses in southeast Raleigh are buried in flood water. Some families in Rochester Heights rebuilt homes three times in one decade. It isn't unusual for me to hear that Rev. Taylor is at his church managing flooding in the church basement after a heavy rainstorm.

Meanwhile, construction projects proliferate throughout downtown Raleigh with promises of growth and expansion. John Kane, the most powerful developer in Raleigh, expands his empire, causing devastating sewage and runoff. And so wastewater rises. Saint Ambrose has done its best to ameliorate the problem on the property. With the help of local organizations, the church installed a rain garden to absorb drainage. But Rev. Taylor tells me it can only do so much good. As long as development continues, the historically Black community purposefully placed in Raleigh's dumping ground will find their homes, churches, and civic center threatened by floodwater. This is the story of white possession of the world, of domination built into the structures of economy and expansion, a colonial story that never ended.

— — —

THE FIRST TIME Judas's name appears in the gospel of John we learn that he is "the devil."

> Because of this many of his disciples turned back and no longer went about with him. So Jesus asked the twelve, "Do you also wish to go away?" Simon Peter answered him, "Lord, to whom can we go? You have the words of eternal life. We have come to believe and know that you are the

> Holy One of God." Jesus answered them, "Did I not choose
> you, the twelve? Yet one of you is a devil." He was speaking
> of Judas son of Simon Iscariot, for he, though one of the
> twelve, was going to betray him. (John 6:66-71)

Jesus does not say Judas is in league with the devil or working with satanic forces. Judas is enacting the role of the devil
in the life of Jesus, tempting Jesus to turn away from the work
of the new order and toward the powers and principalities of
destruction as possession. Even among the people who follow
Jesus, who have seen him heal and cast out demons, who have
received words of life—even here, there is betrayal.

We learn of Judas's status as a perpetrator of the old order
not from Jesus but from the narrator of John, who reveals to us
what the disciples do not know, perhaps what even Judas does
not know. Chrysostom reads into this Jesus' warning against
desertion, a concern he sensed "common among" the disciples,
and not isolated to Judas. Judas's defection to the old order
of Mammon pursues all the disciples. It possessed Peter in his
rejection of Jesus' death by torture on the cross. They are not
safe from this possession by being a part of Jesus' inner circle.

We learn a bit more about Judas's desire for possession in the
Gospels. Judas holds the common purse, from which he was
stealing. And we may be tempted, as scholars have throughout the ages, to construe Judas's thievery as a moral weakness.
Hollis Phelps asks us to turn the questions around. What if,
instead, Judas is a thief because of his access to money?[20] Judas
is taken and possessed by Mammon, the kingdom of Satan. He
gives allegiance to its possibility, and this becomes the source of
his worship. The power of domination and Mammon are one
and the same.

We come to understand this possibility as we read the other significant exchange regarding Judas that is preserved in John's gospel. Jesus visits the home of Mary, Martha, and their brother, Lazarus. While there, Mary brings out an expensive nard, worth a year's wages, and pours it on Jesus' feet. It is extravagant and costly. It is Judas who rebukes her, offering the excuse that this could have been sold and given to the poor. Below his protest is a desire to steal from the common purse that Judas carries for the disciples and Jesus. The power of money is domination—both unruly and deceptive, even to ourselves.

In the end, at the Last Supper, Judas will take a piece of bread and then "Satan entered into him" (John 13:27). Judas becomes the agent for this satanic power of possession and through it he becomes possessed. The world, as Judas has come to believe it must be, will not arrive through this kind of messiah. Until the final destruction of the lord of this possession—Satan—the poor will always be among us.

— — —

JOHN'S GOSPEL CONTRASTS Peter and Judas; in this contrast we see two outcomes for the betrayals of possession and what this could mean for the possession of whiteness in our own time. In John's gospel the last we hear about Judas is that he positions himself among those who will put Jesus on trial. Then Judas drops out of the narrative. We are left with the image of the band of law officials, faces lit by torches, Judas's face another among them. He takes his place among his people, absorbed into the carceral order that will execute Jesus.

But Peter's betrayal is just beginning. After defending Jesus with a sword (and after Jesus' rejection of this violence through the healing of a wounded soldier), Peter finds himself wandering the grounds of the trial complex. Here Peter will be asked three times if he is among Jesus' disciples. And three times Peter will deny his association with Jesus.

We are not told about the three terrible days during which Peter bears this betrayal. But we do know this—Peter returns to the disciples. It is here among them that Mary will find Jesus and announce to Peter the news of the empty tomb. The story of John ends with a meal. John and Jesus eat from the miraculous catch offered by the risen Jesus—the one in whom the abundance of creation is not possession but a gift (John 21).

Three times—one for each of the betrayals—Peter is asked if he will enact this new order with God's people, making a life of love among those whom Jesus loves. Jesus asks, "Do you love me?" To love Jesus is to live within the new order of redemption.

The eradication of whiteness and its power of domination does not depend upon our individual dispositions, feelings, or revelations, even as these are part of the larger work of racial reckoning. Only our collective action toward a renewed order can exorcise the economics of Black exploitation and political oppression that choke out hopes for a future different from our past.

-TWELVE-

The End of Enemies

THE NEW TESTAMENT anticipates an end to enemies. Time functions in such a way that the powers and principalities that trigger havoc on Earth will face a final destruction. God's promises of redemption and peace in Jesus Christ will be fulfilled. The book of Revelation offers a poetic vision of that unfolding, offered to John when he is exiled on the island of Patmos. The good news is that we will not struggle forever.

John's apocalypse ends with a new heaven and new earth. "See, the home of God is among mortals," John proclaims.

> He will dwell with them;
> they will be his peoples,
> and God himself will be with them;
> he will wipe every tear from their eyes.
> Death will be no more;
> mourning and crying and pain will be no more,
> for the first things have passed away. (Revelation 21:3-4)

But before this, before we arrive at the gates of pearl and walls of jasper, before there is no need for sun or moon, before the crystal water flows to the throne of God, the old world turns to fire.

John pens a letter to a community that has survived the destruction of Jerusalem. They continue on as part of a small, oppressed religious minority. Rome charged Christians with intolerance for their rejection of the Roman pantheon that ordered each aspect of social and economic life. Christians refused to worship the false god of peace that was at the heart of the *Pax Romana*. Acts of the Apostles bears witness to the beatings, stonings, imprisonment, and social rejection experienced by members of the early church, and Revelation reflects the trauma of this time. Brian Blount calls Revelation a "mean book" but not one that is mean-spirited.[1] John's meanness emerges from an intense anger at the destruction and death he sees around him. "He envisions a God who means the business of justice and judgment."[2]

Some people read John's revelation as a future story that trumpets the triumph of vengeance. Our enemies, those who act outside of God's commands, meet their end in eternal pain and horror. Eventually the scales will balance as those who prop up the old order are flicked into the lake of eternal fire. With them go death and destruction.

But our desire to position John's poems and hymns as portents of future events with clear victors is theological trickery. Reading Revelation this way is a tactic to deepen a crisis between the church and the world. People are easier to manipulate when they are on the look-out for signs of the end times outside, creeping in to tear us apart. But when I read John's revelation, I don't see a future prophecy. I see the world I know.

In Revelation, the end of the world begins with a scroll. At the earliest stages of the great undoing of earthly life God, the author of creation, opens a seal. In chapter six, we read that four riders on horses emerge from a scroll that opens. The horsemen are not sent or commanded. Instead, we see God wresting control of human violence, unleashing us to the destruction we assail, to "slaughter one another" (Revelation 6:4).

Albrecht Dürer's woodcut depicting the scene of the four horsemen reads this violent undoing into his own time, among his people. His art shows the apocalypse set amidst the backdrop of the Reformation. In his woodcut, Dürer illustrates three warriors riding at the fore. They are not otherworldly. Two appear in the military garb of the Turkish Empire, the geo-political threat to Europe during Dürer's day. The third is a banker or pawnbroker, ready to exploit the poor. As I look at the woodcut, I can imagine horsemen in any time period, as tanks rolling into Tiananmen Square, American helicopters dropping cluster bombs on the thatched roofs of a Vietnamese family, or the U.S. Capitol Police shooting tear gas at peaceful protestors outside the Episcopal church of St. John's near the White House.

In the image that John sees of the horsemen, the warriors on horseback make no distinction between the people they trample and slash. The faithful are not saved from the riders and neither are the wicked. With his tools, Dürer carved into the wood a pompous burgher, a stunned peasant, a seamstress, and a monk—all about to meet a common death. They are bound up in mutual destruction.

— — —

IN 1962 JAMES BALDWIN wrote with the clarity and urgency of John on Patmos, "Letter from a Region in my Mind."[3] Like

Revelation, his essay is saturated in warning and hope for the people of his day. Baldwin writes that there is no retreat from the socio-political space we bear together, one in which Black people, a hundred years after Emancipation, "remain—with the possible exception of the American Indian—the most despised creature[s] in [the] country."[4]

In his letter Baldwin reflects on the apocalypse of racial violence and destruction around him:

> The white man himself is sore in need of new standards, which will release him from his confusion and place him once again in the fruitful communion with the depths of his own being. And I repeat: The price of the liberation of the white people is the liberation of the blacks—the total liberation, in the cities, in the towns, before the law, and in the mind.[5]

"We deeply need each other," Baldwin goes on, "if we really are to become a nation." For Baldwin this will require white people to move beyond an armistice to a kind of maturity. The only freedom for white people, the only way to be released from the "private fears and longing projected onto the Negro," "is to consent, in effect, to become black himself, to become part of that suffering and dancing country that he now watches wistfully from the heights of his lonely power."[6]

Fifty-seven years after Baldwin penned these words, we are still locked in a fierce and formidable racial struggle. Rather than heeding the warning of Baldwin, white supremacy spreads out as self-deception, clamping down on the power slipping from the grasp of white people. Baldwin, like John, warned us of an ordinary apocalypse, seeping in through human destruction.

— — —

BALDWIN WROTE THROUGH the unveiling of white supremacy in the 1960s. In the book of Revelation, John sketches the scene of political and economic exploitation in his day. On the island of Patmos, John shows us the threats of power and violence threatening the region. He uses the image of four warriors on horseback. War is the first of Revelation's horsemen to material- ize from the scroll. He carries a bow and rides a Parthian horse. These instruments of death would doubtless remind the first readers of John's apocalypse of the Parthian forces who were a "nagging reminder about the limits and security that Rome—the region's most powerful empire—could provide."[7] Prospering in the *Pax Romana* was a false hope, and the slippage at the border by invading armies is a sign John places before the churches.

The second rider moves from the external threats of violence to the disruption and violence within their society. In the *Pax Romana*, writes Isaac Villegas, "the people were pacified with a burgeoning economy dependent upon a social order of inden- tured servitude and slavery of foreigners."[8] Worship of this "god of peace" brought new roads and the end of regional conflict. But subjugation of religious minorities and mass crucifixions to stave off insurrection were the sacrifice demanded by *Pax Romana*. In this second rider, Craig Koester hears John's warn- ing "against being lulled into complacency by comfortable con- ditions that pass for peace (Revelation 3:1)."[9] A peace of this kind is built on idolatry and destruction.

In Dürer's woodcut the figures of the horseman draw ever closer. They are layered on the cutting with each rider hurtling in the direction of the viewer. The third rider holds a scale in his hands, the weapon of economic destitution. The seven church- es to whom John writes were a mix of the prosperous and those at the very bottom of the social order. Those who did well in the *Pax Romana* flourished in an economy of exploitation and taxation. Food was widely available. But for the poor, an entire day's labor afforded no more than a small sack of grain. The god of peace worshiped by Rome could not stave off famine from crop failure. This tentative prosperity could be shattered by pestilence or drought, which threatened from the wings.

The closest of Dürer's horseman is a sickly rider on a gaunt horse. While nearest the viewer, he is at the back, the last of the horsemen. He attracts less attention, easy to overlook among the massive stallions towering above with their powerful weapons. This fourth rider is death. Death is the one "given authority" (Revelation 6:8), the specter behind the destruction, the acting force within the *Pax Romana*. We meet death, the true force behind the impotent god of peace, who achieves wealth and prosperity through slavery and sword.

John's vision of the four horsemen is not designed to explain suffering or evil or to help enlighten us about the relationship between God's action and human will. The four horsemen are an admonition, as they are in every age, of the catastrophe human beings bring to creation. There will be few survivors of the old order. If we are unsettled, then John's revelation has done its work.

— — —

IN THE YEARS that followed "Letter from a Region in My Mind," Baldwin grew skeptical of the possibilities of the cooperative and harmonious interracial future he envisioned in his early years. Over the course of a decade, he mourned the assassination of Medgar Evers. He watched as the skin of Black protestors was blasted off with fire hoses in the hands of white police. Martin Luther King Jr. was assassinated. White moderates remained unmoved. Baldwin could no longer believe in an awakening of a national conscience.

He became convinced that white Americans would choose the economic exploitation of capitalism over Black liberation every time, saying,

> The doctrine of white supremacy, which still controls most white people, is itself a stupendous delusion: but to be born black in America is an immediate, a mortal challenge. People who cling to their delusions find it difficult, if not impossible, to learn anything worth learning.[10]

Baldwin continued to affirm that "the truth which frees black people will also free white people, but this is a truth which white people find very difficult to swallow."[11] But if this violence, with its roots in the theft of Black wealth and the restrictions on Black flourishing, could not bring white moderates to action, what would?

Baldwin wrote about how progress in America—progress like the expansion of the railway—conveyed wealth to a few white people even as it robbed the Black community of opportunity. At every turn, as Black people demanded the future that had been stolen from them, white people mounted new and ever more violent opposition. Today we build new jails and hire more police. We gate our communities and elect white supremacists to the highest offices of the land.

Baldwin's earlier writing is a treatise on the impossible wonder of a human community that he believed all people desired to protect from disaster. A decade later he returns to these thoughts: "It is terrible to watch people cling to their captivity and insist on their own destruction. I think black people have always felt this about America, and Americans, and have always seen, spinning above the thoughtless American head, the shape of the wrath to come."[12] To read the apocalypse of John, to live in the world, is to participate in the making of our own destruction and to watch it circle above us.

— — —

IN MOST OF REVELATION, the vengeance we claim to be the fault of God is actually of our own making. John approaches a throne, and as he bitterly weeps, he hears a voice: "Do not weep. See, the Lion of the tribe of Judah, the Root of David, has conquered, so that he can open the scroll and its seven seals" (Revelation 5:5). What John sees does not match the words he hears. On the throne is a Lamb "standing as if it had been slaughtered" (Revelation 5:6). The Lion of Judah is also, somehow, the Lamb who is slain, their identities woven together.

I hold that image through the rest of John's apocalypse. At each juncture we discover a choice to be made. We are asked by John to see ourselves in the seven churches to whom he writes this vision. These questions are asked of people in every generation: will we take our place among the faithful who also become the victims through their active witness against the power of death? Or will we continue to get along within the peace of quietism and conformity?

We lose hold of the power of John's revelation to call us back to taking our place here, within the liberating love of God's power, if we read these words without context. The Bible intends for us to put ourselves among the seven churches to whom this letter is addressed, but this gets lost in the speculation as to who will be on the receiving end of God's retribution. I've found the most valuable readings of John emerge from people who recognize that the horsemen are already raining down their terror.

This was the case for John, who placed the stirrings of apocalypse in his own day. Allan Boesak wrote about his own vision of apartheid South Africa in the grips of a cosmic battle. Boesak, who had no patience for those who would look away from the hostile and oppressive politics of South Africa, mirrored John's vision:

> Jesus came, not simply to pour oil on our wounds or cover up the sinfulness of our world. He came to destroy the works of Satan. He did this not by matching the power of Satan with equal power; not with propaganda or violence; not with the simple, pietistic sentimentality of the sweet, gentle Jesus invented by Western Christianity. He did it by his incarnation, his identification with the poor, the meek, and the lowly; by his engagement in the struggle for God's kingdom of shalom and justice and love, even at the price of his life.[13]

"God is angry," wrote the Dominican Albert Nolan during the apartheid regime. "God is angry, God is absolutely furious about what is being done to the people in South Africa today. . . . The anger of God has become visible for all to see in the anger of the people."[14]

Vengeance as punishment for the wicked may instead be God turning us over to the old order, the destruction of our own creation. This is where we find death—within the logic of retribution. Over and over, Revelation brings our own mutual destruction to culmination. God, in anger, releases us back upon ourselves.

Writing from the midst of the COVID-19 pandemic, its decimation of economies and ruin of human life, we wonder, "Is this the apocalypse?" Catherine Keller and John J. Thatamanil answer, "We hope so."[15] Apocalypse unveils our social order—what we value and what we consider worthless. "Prophecy," write Keller and Thatamanil, "is the poetic unveiling of underlying patterns—patterns of civilization so deep that they may replicate themselves indefinitely, until they bring on some climactic self-destruction."[16] What is being revealed to us in the catastrophe of electoral crisis, in the spread of viral death, and in the Movement for Black lives? We are given another chance to break open our vengeance and to choose our place among the faithful who stand witness to God's liberation of peace.

— — —

REVELATION IS NOT AN EASY BOOK. Its dream code, obvious to its first readers, became a tool to control through fear, from end-time preachers to Christian Zionists. Revelation builds its metaphors on ghastly, misogynistic images. It is a frightening book. But it is preserved for us so that in every generation we awake from our sleep, pulled out of moderation and moved into a form of life where, if we live as Jesus lives, we will stand against the work of death in its brutal and benign forms.

Revelation offers to us, in images and hymns, in metaphors and poems, what we cannot grasp in narrative. In the catastrophe uncoiling in our time, I return to another piece of art. The painters who drew the illuminated manuscript the Saint John's Bible added rainbows throughout the stories of Scripture. In each biblical narrative or prophecy where life is stressed by fear or war, somewhere in the picture the artists drew the hues of a rainbow. It is there among the wreckage—a promise.

But these signs of hope burst into every frame of the illuminations for the book of Revelation. They form buildings and pour from bloodstained war scenes. Within the destruction, the artists embedded God's covenant with Noah:

> "When the bow is in the clouds, I will see it and remember the everlasting covenant between God and every living creature of all flesh that is on the earth." God said to Noah, "This is the sign of the covenant that I have established between me and all flesh that is on the earth." (Genesis 9:16-17)

We do not know how we as people will bring destruction upon ourselves or the ways God will release us back to our violence. But this Word, this sign of hope, is also true.

In his early letter, still fresh with hope for the civil rights movement, James Baldwin reflected on the stories of a world-ending apocalypse in both Muslim and Christian traditions:

> I wondered, when the vengeance was achieved, *What will happen to all that beauty then?* I could also see that the intransigence and ignorance of the white world might make that vengeance inevitable—a vengeance that does not really depend on, and cannot really be executed by, any person or organization, and that cannot be prevented by any police force or army: historical vengeance, a cosmic vengeance, based on the law that we recognize when we say, "Whatever goes up must come down."[17]

I imagine this is the vengeance that is galloping toward us. We hear the rumbling through history, the ground shaking beneath us.

How will the world end today?
And *what will happen to all the beauty?*

A Sermonic Epilogue

FOR MOST OF MY LIFE I read the Beatitudes as instruction, a mild if not righteous scolding. These words of Jesus changed when I began to read them as description rather than prescription.

Different versions of Scripture translate "blessed" in the Beatitudes, conveying a range of ways for us to interpret these verses. One says, "Happy are those." Another: "You're blessed." Or "Blessed be." But another way to translate "blessed" is "Congratulations!" Or "Good on you!" The Greek word *blessed* celebrates and affirms people as they are. Jesus describes not future behaviors, expectations of the people who hear them, but the acknowledgment of their current reality.

The peasants before Jesus—fishermen and farmers, beggars and widows—are forced down, weighted by economic terror and political repression. The lives into which they were born keep them at the margins of political, social, and economic power. Jesus comes to them and says, "You are as you ought

199

to be. You, you alone, are the ones who make up the kingdom of God." The invitation to follow Jesus isn't to accept the way things are. The poor, the dispossessed, and those on the margins are embedded in the grain of God's justice. These are God's beloved.

THE AUTHOR PETER WOHLLEBEN is an arborist who tells the story of trees and how their lives are interconnected in kinship systems. Older mother-trees, he writes, will deprive their saplings of sun to help them not grow too quickly, which shortens their life span. Some trees protect one another by emitting gas that sends a warning of danger. Through "chemical, hormonal and slow-pulsing electrical signals" they communicate alarm and distress.[1]

The Hidden Life of Trees is a remarkable book that pulled me out of an assumption about "survival of the fittest" ingrained in me by my meager scientific training in high school. I was taught that the way the world works, the way it survives, is by one creature clobbering another, looking out for itself, and sacrificing the weakest so that the strong can populate the Earth. But when Wohlleben looks at trees he sees something else. He writes, "But isn't that how evolution works? you ask. The survival of the fittest? Trees would just shake their heads—or rather their crowns. Their well-being depends on their community, and when the supposedly feeble trees disappear, the others lose as well."[2]

Deeply embedded in the cycles of nature is a quiet form of a life echoing back the words that Jesus speaks. This is a good life: to look out for one another to see the weakest and most vulnerable as necessary for the good life. It's a good life to forge ahead toward forgiveness in a world that demands revenge. It's a good life to let go of oppression and to refrain from dominating other people. It's a good life to seek reconciliation instead of persisting in our rightness or looking for a window to exact retribution.

If we live out this good life, we'll start to look different from everyone else. It will get you into trouble, Jesus tells the people listening to him. It may even get you killed, one day. But the people who need to find you will be able to make their way to you, because you'll be like a lit-up city on a hill.

In a world poisoned by light pollution, it's hard to grasp the full cadence of this metaphor. But a Nicaraguan campesino named Macelino once described what it meant to see a city like this, in the 1970s on Lake Nicaragua, far from the large industrial centers where electricity is plentiful. "A lit-up city that's on top of a hill can be seen from far away, as we can see the lights of San Miguelito from very far away when we're rowing at night on the lake," he writes. "A city is a great union of people, and as there are a lot of houses together we see a lot of light. And that's the way our community will be. It will be seen lighted from far away, if it is united in love."[3]

The Bible is a powerful weapon in the hands of oppressors. It always has been. But Matthew writes these words for the poor, for the ones who have been told, "There's no place for you here." Jesus sits beside them and says, "You are in the good life, in the perfect place, the good life for you and the good life for others." And when these people find one another, when they are united in love, Jesus' love begins to unfold all around us. You are in the good life. Blessed are you.

Notes

EPIGRAPH

1 *The Revised Grail Psalms: A Liturgical Psalter*, prepared by the Benedictine Monks of Conception Abbey (Collegeville, MN: Liturgical Press, 2012).

PREFACE

1 I found a helpful summation of Tanner's ecclesiology in Brad East, "An Undefensive Presence: The Mission and Identity of the Church in Kathryn Tanner and John Howard Yoder," *Scottish Journal of Theology* 68, no. 3 (August 2015): 327–344.

2 Kathryn Tanner, *Christ the Key* (New York: Cambridge University Press, 2010), vii.

3 Kathryn Tanner, "Towards a New Theology of Confirmation," *Anglican Theological Review* 88, no. 1 (Winter 2006): 93.

4 Kathryn Tanner, *Theories of Culture: A New Agenda for Theology* (Minneapolis: Fortress Press, 1997), 42.

5 Tanner, *Theories of Culture*, 112.

6 Tanner, 123 (italics removed).

7 James Cone, *A Black Theology of Liberation* (New York: Lippincott, 1970), 11.

8 "The #BlackLivesMatter Movement: Marches and Tweets for Healing," NPR, June 9, 2015 https://www.npr.org/2015/06/09/

412862459/the-blacklivesmatter-movement-marches-and-tweets
-for-healing.

9 Alicia Garza, "A Herstory of the #BlackLivesMatter Movement,"
The Feminist Wire, October 7, 2014, https://www.thefeministwire
.com/2014/10/blacklivesmatter-2/.

10 Laura Flanders, "Building Movements Without Shedding
Differences: Alicia Garza of #BlackLivesMatter," *Truthout*, March
24, 2015, https://truthout.org/video/building-movements-with
out-shedding-differences-alicia-garza/.

11 Karl Barth, *Church Dogmatics*, trans. G.W. Bromiley, vol. 4, part
3.2, *The Doctrine of Reconciliation* (London: T&T Clark International, 2004), 826.

12 In Peter Dula, *Cavell, Companionship, and Christian Theology*
(Oxford: Oxford University Press, 2010).

CHAPTER ONE

1 Terri Blom Crocker, *The Christmas Truce: Myth, Memory, and the
First World War* (Lexington, KY: University of Kentucky Press,
2015), 1.

2 Crocker, *The Christmas Truce*, 1–10.

3 "German sailors begin to mutiny," History, https://www.history
.com/this-day-in-history/german-sailors-begin-to-mutiny.

4 Gratitude to Benjamin Isaak-Krauß for drawing to my attention
the anti-war movements of World War I.

5 Rowan Williams, "Overcoming Political Tribalism," *ABC Religion
& Ethics*, October 2, 2019, https://www.abc.net.au/religion/
rowan-williams-overcoming-political-tribalism/11566242.

6 Williams, "Overcoming Political Tribalism."

7 Williams.

8 Williams.

9 Kenya Young, "A Black Mother Reflects On Giving Her 3 Sons
'The Talk'. . . Again and Again," interview by Sam Sanders, *It's
Been a Minute*, NPR, June 28, 2020, https://www.npr.org/2020/
06/28/882383372/a-black-mother-reflects-on-giving-her-3-sons
-the-talk-again-and-again.

10 Young, "A Black Mother Reflects."

11 I am not making a definitive claim on the definition of *enemy*.
Instead, this is my attempt to offer a definition that will guide
how I made decisions on what to include in this book as well as
the way we address this particular relationship.

12 Alicia Garza, "A Herstory of the #BlackLivesMatter Movement," *The Feminist Wire*, October 7, 2014, https://www.thefeministwire .com/2014/10/blacklivesmatter-2/.

13 Garza, "A Herstory."

14 Garza.

15 Amanda Aguilar Shank, "Beyond Firing: How Do We Create Community-wide Accountability for Sexual Harassment in Our Movements?" in *Beyond Survival: Strategies and Stories from the Transformative Justice Movement*, eds. Ejeris Dixon and Leah Lakshmi Piepzna-Samarasinha (Chico, CA: AK Press, 2020), chap. 3.

CHAPTER TWO

1 Keeanga-Yamahtta Taylor, "Black Feminism and the Combahee River Collective," *Monthly Review,* January 1, 2019, https:// monthlyreview.org/2019/01/01/black-feminism-and-the -combahee-river-collective/.

2 Keeanga-Yamahtta Taylor, ed., *How We Get Free: Black Feminism and the Combahee River Collective* (Chicago, Haymarket Books, 2017), 18.

3 Taylor, *How We Get Free*, 18.

4 Taylor, 61.

5 Paulo Freire, *The Politics of Education: Culture, Power and Liberation* (Westport, CT: Bergin & Garvey, 1985), 122.

6 Kelly Brown Douglas, *The Black Christ*, 25th anniv. ed. (Maryknoll, NY: Orbis Books, 2019), introduction, Kindle.

7 Kelly Brown Douglas, "The Race of It All: Conversations Between a Mother and Her Son," in *Parenting as Spiritual Practice and Source for Theology: Mothering Matters*, eds. Claire Bischoff, Elizabeth O'Donnell Gandolfo, and Annie Hardison-Moody (Cham, Switzerland: Palgrave MacMillan, 2017), 30.

CHAPTER THREE

1 Arthur Mondale, "Inmates Will Not Be Released," Southern Coalition for Social Justice, August 31, 2010, https://www .southerncoalition.org/inmates-will-not-be-released/.

2 Jeremiah Wright, "The Day of Jerusalem's Fall (September 2001)" in *Preaching with Sacred Fire: An Anthology of African American Sermons, 1750 to the Present*, eds. Martha Simmons and Frank A. Thomas (New York: W.W. Norton, 2010), 855–856. Transcription

of one phrase in Wright's audio has been corrected based on "The Day of Jerusalem's Fall," Blakfacts, March 28, 2008, https://blakfacts.blogspot.com/2008/03/day-of-jerusalems-fall.html.

3 While the Hebrew utilizes masculine pronouns, it can be a helpful exercise for us to release the gendered language of the psalms, opening our imaginations to how these psalms offer space for a variety of responses to violence in our own time, including violence against women and LGBTQ people.

4 Erich Zenger, *A God of Vengeance? Understanding the Psalms of Divine Wrath*, tr. Linda M. Maloney (Louisville, KY: Westminster John Knox Press, 1996), 3.

5 C. S. Lewis, *Reflections on the Psalms* (New York: Harcourt, Brace and Company, 1958), 20–22.

6 In the narrative in which Judas is replaced as one of the twelve disciples (Acts 1:16-20), Peter references Psalm 109:8.

7 Stanley Meisler, "The Massacre in El Mozote," in *Thinking Clearly: Cases in Journalistic Decision-Making*, eds. Tom Rosenstiel and Amy S. Mitchell (New York: Columbia University Press, 2003), 114.

8 J. Clinton McCann, Jr., *A Theological Introduction to the Book of Psalms: The Psalms as Torah* (Nashville, TN: Abingdon, 1993), 119–120.

9 Herbert McCabe, *God, Christ, and Us* (London: Continuum, 2005), 8.

10 McCabe, *God, Christ, and Us*, 8.

11 Mark Adams, "The Valley of the Shadow of Death is Near Douglas, Arizona," Presbyterian Church (U.S.A.) Presbyterian Mission, September 23, 2019, https://www.presbyterianmission.org/story/healing-our-borders/.

CHAPTER FOUR

1 Beverly W. Harrison, "The Power of Anger in the Work of Love: Christian Ethics for Women and Other Strangers," in *Korean American Women: Towards Self-Realization,* ed. Inn Sook Lee (Eugene, OR: Wipf and Stock, 2009), 163.

2 Willie Jennings, "My Anger, God's Righteous Indignation," interview by Evan Rosa, *For the Life of the World,* Yale Center for Faith & Culture, June 2, 2020, https://for-the-life-of-the-world-yale-center-for-faith-culture.simplecast.com/episodes/my-anger-gods-righteous-indignation-willie-jennings-response-to-the-death-of-george-floyd-FXkkWh9b/transcript.

3 Jennings, "My Anger."

4 Jennings.

5 Choe Song-Hun, "Korea Opens Dark Chapter of History," *New York Times*, April 5, 2005, https://www.nytimes.com/2005/04/05/world/asia/korea-opens-dark-chapter-of-history.html.

6 Wonchul Shin, "Reimagining Anger in Christian Traditions: Anger as a Moral Virtue for the Flourishing of the Oppressed in Political Resistance," *Religions* 11, no. 5 (May 14, 2020): 6.

7 Shin, "Reimagining Anger," 9.

8 Shin, 12.

9 Shin, 9.

10 Jennings, "My Anger."

11 Audre Lorde, *Sister Outsider: Essays and Speeches of Audre Lorde* (New York: Penguin Books, 2020), 115.

12 Lorde, *Sister Outsider*, 115.

13 Lorde, 118.

14 Lorde, 118.

15 Lorde, 118.

16 Thomas Aquinas, *Summa Theologiae,* 2nd ed., trans. Fathers of the English Dominican Province, ed. Kevin Knight, New Advent, 2017, 2–2.158.8, https://www.newadvent.org/summa/3158.htm.

17 Ian McFarland, *The Word Made Flesh: A Theology of the Incarnation* (Louisville, KY: Westminster John Knox Press, 2019), 12.

18 Karl Barth, *Dogmatics in Outline* (London: SCM Classics, 2007), chap. 23, Kindle.

19 Barth, *Dogmatics in Outline.*

20 Sara Kershnar, Staci Haines, Gillian Harkins, Alan Greig, Cindy Wiesner, Mich Levy, Palak Shah, Mimi Kim, and Jesse Carr, *Toward Transformative Justice: A Liberatory Approach to Child Sexual Abuse and Other Forms of Intimate and Community Violence* (Generation FIVE, 2007), http://www.usprisonculture.com/blog/wp-content/uploads/2012/03/G5_Toward_Transformative_Justice.pdf.

21 Mia Mingus, "Transformative Justice: A Brief Description," *Leaving Evidence* (blog), January 9, 2019, https://leavingevidence.wordpress.com/2019/01/09/transformative-justice-a-brief-description/.

22 Ejeris Dixon, "Building Community: Practical Steps Towards Liberatory Transformation" in *Beyond Survival: Strategies and Stories from the Transformative Justice Movement,* eds. Ejeris Dixon

and Leah Lakshmi Piepzna-Samarasinha (Chico, CA: AK Press, 2020), chap. 1, Kindle.

CHAPTER FIVE

1 Epictetus, *The Discourses of Epictetus with the Encheiridion and Fragments, Vol. 1,* tr. George Long (London: George Bell and Sons, 1891), 16.

2 *Berakhot* 61b.

3 John A. Darr, *Herod the Fox: Audience Criticism and Lukan Characterization* (Sheffield, UK: Sheffield University Press, 1998), 179.

4 Isaac Villegas, "The Politics of Mary: A Sermon on Luke 1:55-56," *Vision: A Journal for Church and Theology* 18, no. 1 (Spring 2017): 66–67.

5 Raniero Cantalamessa, *The Mystery of Christmas: A Commentary on the Magnificat, Gloria, Nunc Dimittis,* trans. Frances Lonergan (Collegeville, MN: Liturgical Press, 1988), 21.

6 Joel B. Green, *The Gospel of Luke* (Grand Rapids, MI: Wm. B. Eerdmans Publishing, 1997), 104.

7 Obery M. Hendricks, Jr., *The Politics of Jesus: Rediscovering the True Revolutionary Nature of Jesus' Teachings and How They Have Been Corrupted* (New York: Three Leaves Press, 2006), 61.

8 Hendricks, *The Politics of Jesus,* 61.

9 Kwok Pui-lan. "Mercy Amba Oduyoye and African Women's Theology," *Journal of Feminist Studies in Religion* 20, no. 1 (Spring 2004): 7–22.

10 Elina Vuola, "*La Morenita* on Skis: Women's Popular Marian Piety and Feminist Research on Religion" in *The Oxford Handbook of Feminist Theology,* eds. Mary McClintock Fulkerson and Sheila Briggs (Oxford: Oxford University Press, 2012), 518.

11 See Amy G. Remensnyder, *La Conquistadora: The Virgin Mary at War and Peace in the Old and New Worlds* (Oxford: Oxford University Press, 2014).

12 Elina Vuola, *Limits of Liberation: Feminist Theology and the Ethics of Poverty and Reproduction* (London: Sheffield Academic Press, 2002), 175.

13 Jennifer Schirmer, "The Seeking of Truth and the Gendering of Consciousness" in *Viva: Women and Popular Protest in Latin America,* eds. Sarah A. Radcliffe and Sallie Westwood (London: Routledge, 1995), 36.

14 Susan Connelly, "The Magnificat as Social Document," *Compass* 48, no. 4 (Summer 2014): 8.

15 Willem Oliver and Erna Oliver, "Regina Mundi: Serving the Liberation Movement in South Africa," *HTS Teologiese Studies/ Theological Studies* 72, no.1 (2016). https://doi.org/10.4102/hts .v72i1.3409.

CHAPTER SIX

1   Daniel W. Hodge, "No Church in the Wild: Missiological Education in a Post-Civil Rights Era" (paper, Association of Professors of Mission Annual Meeting, Wheaton, IL June 15–16, 2017), https://place.asburyseminary.edu/cgi/viewcontent.cgi?article= 1153&context=firstfruitspapers.

2   James Cone, *God of the Oppressed* (Maryknoll, NY: Orbis Books, 1997), chap. 9, Kindle.

3   Paulo Freire, *Pedagogy of the Oppressed* (New York: Bloomsbury Press, 2012), 48.

4   Lori Brandt Hale, "From Loving Enemies to Acting Responsibly: Forgiveness in the Life and Theology of Dietrich Bonhoeffer," *Word & World* 27, no. 1 (Winter 2007): 79.

5   Dietrich Bonhoeffer, *Life Together* (London: SCM Press, 2015), 8.

6   Bonhoeffer, *Life Together*, 241.

7   Dietrich Bonhoeffer, *Ethics* (New York: Simon & Schuster, 1995), 33.

8   Brian Bantum, "Mulatto Theology: Race, Discipleship, and *Inter-racial* Existence,"(PhD diss., Duke University, 2009), 182, https:// dukespace.lib.duke.edu/dspace/bitstream/handle/10161/1185/D_ Bantum_Brian_a_200904.pdf?sequence=1&isAllowed=y).

9   Reinhold Niebuhr, "Death of a Martyr," *Christianity and Crisis*, June 25, 1945, repr., "Political Questions Are Not Irrelevant to Faith: A Reflection on Dietrich Bonhoeffer's Martyrdom," *Providence*, August 4, 2020, https://providencemag.com/2020/08/ political-questions-irrelevant-faith-reflection-dietrich-bonhoeffer -martyrdom/.

10 Karl Marx, *Marx on Religion,* ed. John Raines (Philadelphia: Temple University Press, 2002), 240.

11 Helmut Thielicke, *Life Can Begin Again: Sermons on the Sermon on the Mount,* tr. John W. Doberstein (Eugene, OR: Wipf and Stock, 2003), xiv.

12 Audre Lorde, *Sister Outsider: Essays and Speeches of Audre Lorde* (New York: Penguin Books, 2020), 102.

13 Audre Lorde, *Sister Outsider*, 103.

14 Rowan Williams, "End of War" in *Dissent from the Homeland: Essays after September 11,* eds. Stanley Hauerwas and Frank Lentricchia (Durham, NC: Duke University Press, 2003), 29.

15 Williams, "End of War," 29.

16 Williams, 29.

17 James Baldwin, "Letter from a Region in My Mind," *New Yorker*, November 17, 1962, https://www.newyorker.com/magazine/1962/11/17/letter-from-a-region-in-my-mind.

18 John Calvin, *John: The Crossway Classical Commentaries* (Wheaton, IL: Crossway Books, 1994), 205.

19 Karl Barth, *The Epistle to the Romans* (Oxford: Oxford University Press, 1968), 473.

CHAPTER SEVEN

1 Andrew Milne, "Ann Atwater Pushed to Integrate Her City's Schools—And Got a Klansman to Join Her in the Fight," *All That's Interesting*, August 13, 2019, https://allthatsinteresting.com/ann-atwater.

2 See Gene Pranger, *HopeFULL: Creating and Maintaining Positive Momentum in the Real World* (Sandy, UT: Positive IQ, 2017) chap. 5, Kindle.

3 Osha Gray Davidson, *The Best of Enemies: Race and Redemption in the New South* (Chapel Hill: University of North Carolina Press, 2007), 217.

4 E.P. Sanders, *Jesus and Judaism* (Philadelphia: Fortress Press, 1985), 252–255.

5 Carolyn Osiek and David L. Balch, *Families in the New Testament World: Households and House Churches* (Lousiville, KY: Westminster John Knox Press, 1997), 42.

6 Jeremy Punt, "Human Dignity, Families, and Violence" in *Fragile Dignity: Intercontexual Conversations on Scriptures, Family, and Violence,* eds. L. Juliana Claassens and Klaas Spronk (Atlanta, Society of Biblical Literature, 2013), 131.

7 Linn Marie Tonstad, *Queer Theology: Beyond Apologetics* (Eugene, OR: Cascade Books, 2018), 81.

8 Tonstad, *Queer Theology*, 81.

9 Osiek and Balch, *Families*, 49.

10 Osiek and Balch, 49.

11 R.T. France, *The Gospel of Matthew* (Grand Rapids, MI: Wm.

B. Eerdmans Publishing, 2007), 243. France also notes that the Mishnah later allowed for property oaths to be waived. While Jesus condemns an act that is happening among a few people within a small sect of Judaism, the larger tradition of Judaism mediated the conflict between this form of property oath and the fifth commandment.

12 See Ecclesiasticus 3:12–16.

13 Justo González, "Christian Ethics in the Context of the Church as *Familia*: Reflections on the Work of Ismael García," *Insights* 127 no. 1 (Fall 2012): 25, http://www.austinseminary.edu/uploaded/about_us/pdf/insights/insights_fall_12.pdf.

14 González, "Church as *Familia*," 25.

15 Ada María Isasi-Díaz, *La Lucha Continues: Mujerista Theology* (Maryknoll, NY: Orbis Books, 2004), 248.

16 Isasi-Díaz, *La Lucha Continues*, 248.

17 Isasi-Díaz, 251.

CHAPTER EIGHT

1 See Amy-Jill Levine's *The Misunderstood Jew: The Church and the Scandal of the Jewish Jesus* (New York: HarperCollins Publishers, 2007).

2 Melissa Buyer-Witman, *Mishkan HaNefesh for Youth: A Machzor for Youth and Families* (New York: CCAR Press, 2018), 147.

3 See Lori Baron, Jill Hicks-Keeton, and Matthew Thiessen, eds., *The Ways That Often Parted: Essays in Honor of Joel Marcus* (Atlanta: SBL Press, 2018).

4 James VanderKam, *The Dead Sea Scrolls and the Bible* (Grand Rapids, MI: Wm. B. Eerdmans Publishing, 2012), 108.

5 Joel Marcus, *Mark 1–8* (New Haven, CT: Yale University Press), 144.

6 Daniel Boyarin, *The Jewish Gospels: The Story of the Jewish Christ* (New York: New Press, 2013), 104.

7 Boyarin, *Jewish Gospels*, 133.

8 Boyarin, 133.

9 Matt Thiessen, *Jesus and the Forces of Death: The Gospels' Portrayal of Ritual Impurity Within First-Century Judaism* (Grand Rapids, MI: Baker Academic, 2020), 11.

10 Thiessen, *Forces of Death*, 179.

11 *Sanhedrin 88b*.

12 *Berakhot 10a*.

CHAPTER NINE

1   Ariel Edwards-Levy, "In 1968, Nearly a Third of Americans Said MLK Brought His Assassination On Himself" *Huffpost*, April 4, 2018, https://www.huffpost.com/entry/in-1968-nearly-a-third-of -americans-said-mlk-brought-his-killing-on-himself_n_ 5ac51373e4b0aacd15b7d37b.

2   Martin Luther King Jr., "Letter from a Birmingham Jail," in *Gospel of Freedom: Martin Luther King, Jr.'s Letter from Birmingham Jail and the Struggle That Changed a Nation*, ed. Jonathan Rieder (New York: Bloomsbury Press, 2013), 181.

3   Anna Elisabetta Galeotti, "Do We Need Toleration as a Moral Virtue?" in *Toleration, Neutrality, and Democracy*, eds. Dario Castigilone and Catriona McKinnon (Berlin: Springer Science+ Business Media, 2003), 60.

4   For more on the socioeconomics of the Weak and the Strong in 1 Corinthians see Dale Martin's *The Corinthian Body* (New Haven, CT: Yale University Press, 1999).

5   Danté Stewart, "As a Black Person, I'm Done Helping White Christians Feel Better about Race," *Washington Post*, July 13, 2020, https://www.washingtonpost.com/outlook/2020/07/13/ black-pastor-white-churches/.

6   Stewart, "I'm Done Helping."

7   Samuel Wells, "Shaking the Dust," *Faith & Leadership*, July 29, 2013, https://faithandleadership.com/samuel-wells-shaking-dust.

CHAPTER TEN

1   "The Black Manifesto at the Riverside Church," Archives Exhibit, Riverside Church in the City of New York, https://www.trcnyc. org/blackmanifesto/. Accessed: 7/10/20.

2   James Forman, "The Black Manifesto: I Introduction: Total Control as the Only Solution to the Economic Problems of Black People," *The Review of Black Political Economy*, March 1, 1970, https://doi.org/10.1007/BF03037541.

3   Tobin Miller Shearer, "Money, Sex, and Power: The Black Manifesto and the Minority Ministries Council," *Anabaptist Historians*, April 13, 2017, https://anabaptisthistorians.org/2017/04/13/ money-sex-and-power-the-black-manifesto-and-the-minority -ministries-council/.

4   Melissa Phruksachart, "The Literature of White Liberalism," *Boston Review*, August 21, 2020, http://bostonreview.net/race/ melissa-phruksachart-literature-white-liberalism.

5 Ta-Nehisi Coates, "The Case for Reparations," *The Atlantic*, June 2014, https://www.theatlantic.com/magazine/archive/2014/06/the-case-for-reparations/361631/.

6 Philip Goodchild, *Credit and Faith* (London: Rowman & Littlefield International, 2019), 31.

7 Goodchild, *Credit and Faith*, 31.

8 Goodchild, 31.

9 Goodchild, 21.

10 Philip Goodchild, *Theology of Money* (Durham, NC: Duke University Press, 2009), 205.

11 Hollis Phelps, *Jesus and the Politics of Mammon*, (Eugene, OR: Wipf and Stock, 2019), 133.

12 Phelps, *Politics of Mammon*, 136.

CHAPTER ELEVEN

1 Chanequa Walker-Barnes, *I Bring the Voices of My People: A Womanist Vision for Racial Reconciliation* (Grand Rapids, MI: Wm. B. Eerdmans Publishing, 2019), chap. 3, Kindle.

2 Sara Ahmed, "Declarations of Whiteness: The Non-Performativity of Anti-Racism," *Borderlands* 3 no. 2, 2004.

3 Willie Jennings, "To Be a Christian Intellectual," *Yale Divinity School*, October 30, 2015, https://divinity.yale.edu/news/willie-jennings-be-christian-intellectual.

4 Jennings, "Christian Intellectual."

5 Walker-Barnes, *Womanist Vision*, chap. 3.

6 M. Eugene Boring, *Mark: A Commentary* (Louisville, KY: Westminster John Knox Press, 2006), 108.

7 Walker-Barnes, *Womanist Vision*, chap. 3.

8 See Sherrilyn Ifill, *On the Courthouse Lawn: Confronting the Legacy of Lynching in the 21st Century* (Boston: Beacon Press, 2018).

9 James Cone, *The Cross and the Lynching Tree* (Maryknoll, NY: Orbis Books, 2011), xiv.

10 Sherrilyn A. Ifill, "Creating a Truth and Reconciliation Commission for Lynching," *Law & Inequality* 21, no. 2 (2003): 269.

11 Equal Justice Initiative, "Lynching in America: Confronting the Legacy of Racial Terror" (3rd ed., 2017). https://lynchinginamerica.eji.org/report/

12 Ifill, "Truth and Reconciliation," 263.

13 Equal Justice Initiative, "Lynching in America."

14 W.E.B. Du Bois, *Black Reconstruction in America 1860–1880*

(New York: Atheneum, 1992), 700.

15 See Jonathan M. Metzl, *Dying of Whiteness: How the Politics of Racial Resentment is Killing America's Heartland* (New York: Basic Books, 2019).

16 W.E.B. Du Bois, *Darkwater: Voices From Within the Veil* (Oxford: Oxford University Press, 2014), 16.

17 Ella Myers, "Beyond the Wages of Whiteness: Du Bois on the Irrationality of Antiblack Racism" *Items: Insights from the Social Sciences*, March 21, 2017. https://items.ssrc.org/reading-racial-conflict/beyond-the-wages-of-whiteness-du-bois-on-the-irrationality-of-antiblack-racism/.

18 W.E.B. DuBois, *Dusk of Dawn: An Essay Towards An Autobiography of Race Concept* (Oxford: Oxford University Press, 2007), 86.

19 See Willie Jennings, *The Christian Imagination: Theology and the Origins of Race* (New Haven: Yale University Press, 2011).

20 Hollis Phelps, *Jesus and the Politics of Mammon* (Eugene, OR: Cascade Books, 2019), 76–77.

CHAPTER TWELVE

1 Brian K. Blount, *Revelation: A Commentary* (Louisville, KY: Westminster John Knox Press, 2009), 1.

2 Blount, *Revelation*, 2.

3 James Baldwin's essay in the *The New Yorker* was republished as "Down at the Cross: Letter from a Region in My Mind." For this book I'm utilizing his original essay from *The New Yorker.* https://www.newyorker.com/magazine/1962/11/17/letter-from-a-region-in-my-mind.

4 Baldwin, "Region in My Mind."

5 Baldwin.

6 Baldwin.

7 Craig R. Koester, *Revelation and the End of All Things* (Grand Rapids: Wm. B. Eerdmans Publishing, 2001), 84.

8 Isaac Villegas, "From Nonresistance to Anti-Violence," in *The Mennonite* (August 2020), 35.

9 Koester, *Revelation*, 84.

10 James Baldwin, *No Name in the Streets* (New York: Vintage International, 2000), 128–129.

11 Baldwin, *No Name*, 129.

12 Baldwin, 195.

13 Allan Boesak, *Comfort and Protest: The Apocalypse from a South African Perspective* (Philadelphia: Westminster Press, 1987), 88.

14 Albert Nolan, *God in South Africa: The Challenge of the Gospel* (Cape Town: David Phillip, 1988), 105.

15 Catherine Keller and John J. Thatamanil, "Is This an Apocalypse? We Certainly Hope So—You Should Too," *ABC Religion & Ethics*, April 15, 2020, https://www.abc.net.au/religion/catherine-keller-and-john-thatamanil-why-we-hope-this-is-an-apo/12151922.

16 Keller and Thatamanil, "Is This an Apocalypse?"

17 Baldwin, "Region in My Mind."

EPILOGUE

1 Peter Wohlleben, *The Hidden Life of Trees: What They Feel, How They Communicate; Discoveries from a Secret World* (New York: HarperCollins, 2002), 118.

2 Wohlleben, *Hidden Life of Trees*, 118.

3 Ernesto Cardenal, ed. *The Gospel in Solentiname* (Eugene, OR: Wipf and Stock, 2010), 96.

The Author

MELISSA FLORER-BIXLER is a writer and pastor with degrees from Duke University and Princeton Theological Seminary. As pastor of Raleigh Mennonite Church in North Carolina, she and her ministry have been featured in *The Atlantic* and *Sojourners*. Her writing can be found in *Geez Magazine*, *Christian Century*, *Faith & Leadership*, *Anabaptist World*, *Anabaptist Witness*, *Vision*, and *The Mennonite*. She is the author of *Fire by Night: Finding God in the Pages of the Old Testament*. Florer-Bixler serves on the board of Friends of L'Arche North Carolina, a community for people with and without intellectual disabilities who live in community. She also works with a strategy team to build broad-based community organizing in Wake County and serves on the Human Relations Commission for the City of Raleigh. Florer-Bixler lives with her husband and three children in Raleigh, North Carolina.